THE LOO LEDGER

A
Guest Book
for the Bathroom

RECORD YOUR THOUGHTS FROM THE THRONE

STERLING
New York

Introduction

Hello, guest! You may find it weird that there's a jar of pens in the bathroom, or weirder still that you are expected to leave your mark in this guest book during your visit. But is it any weirder than reading a book of the 1,000 crappiest potty jokes while you relieve yourself? Ok, maybe, but you'll find those here too—just flip to the back of this book.

More than just tracking the comings and *goings* of all you lovely people, this ledger is for your entertainment because nothing is more embarrassing than a video on your phone blasting at full volume when you're trying to be subtle. Bottom line: everybody poops, so you might as well make the most of it. Sit down, take a load off (or, you know, drop one), flip to a new page, and grab a pen! Don't forget to flush with mercy, spray with zeal, and wash your hands with warm water and soap (please!).

Have a nice poop!

Love,

_____

THANKS FOR DROPPING BY

YOUR NAME:

....

IF YOU'RE NOT HERE TO SEE A MAN ABOUT A HORSE, WHAT BROUGHT YOU TO THE LOO?

☐ Just a wiz, lay off!
☐ Freshening up my make-up
☐ Escaping the crowd
☐ Letting out a secret fart or two
☐ Taking a self-guided tour
☐ Signing this stinkin' book
☐ Making a pit stop (ahem, reapplying deodorant—don't be nosy)
☐ Other:

....

DOO DOO-DLE

Draw a cute poo!

CREATE AND NAME YOUR DREAM BATHROOM FRESHENER SCENT

.... +
(Part of Speech)

.... +
(Part of Speech)

.... =
(Part of Speech)

MOVEMENT METER

How was your poop?

RATE YOUR POOP ON THE SCALE BELOW WITH A HAND-DRAWN POOP EMOJI:

 Dreadfully Dumpy

 Positively Poo-tastic

TOILET PAPER SUPER BOWL

Choose your battle!

CIRCLE ONE:
* SOFTEST FEEL *   * CATCHIEST JINGLE *   * HARDEST WORKING *

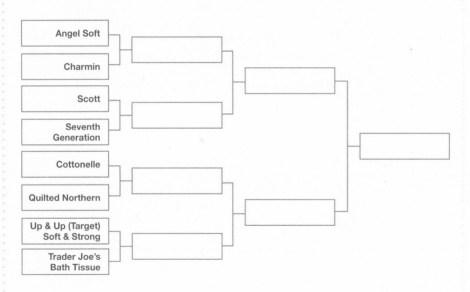

- Angel Soft
- Charmin
- Scott
- Seventh Generation
- Cottonelle
- Quilted Northern
- Up & Up (Target) Soft & Strong
- Trader Joe's Bath Tissue

.... , you're on a roll!

Winning Team

QUALITY ASS-URANCE

How did we doo-doo?

RATE YOUR EXPERIENCE ON A SCALE OF
1 TO 5, 5 MEANING EXTREMELY SATISFIED.

Cleanliness ☆ ☆ ☆ ☆ ☆

Aesthetics ☆ ☆ ☆ ☆ ☆

Toilet Paper ☆ ☆ ☆ ☆ ☆

Spray/SoapScent ☆ ☆ ☆ ☆ ☆

Privacy ☆ ☆ ☆ ☆ ☆

Ventilation ☆ ☆ ☆ ☆ ☆

Plunger Power ☆ ☆ ☆ ☆ ☆

THANKS FOR DROPPING BY

THANKS FOR DROPPING BY

YOUR NAME:

....

IF YOU'RE NOT HERE TO SEE A MAN ABOUT A HORSE, WHAT BROUGHT YOU TO THE LOO?

☐ Just a wiz, lay off!

☐ Freshening up my make-up

☐ Escaping the crowd

☐ Letting out a secret fart or two

☐ Taking a self-guided tour

☐ Signing this stinkin' book

☐ Making a pit stop (ahem, reapplying deodorant—don't be nosy)

☐ Other:

....

....

DOO DOO-DLE

Draw a cute poo!

CREATE AND NAME YOUR DREAM BATHROOM FRESHENER SCENT

.... +
(Part of Speech)

.... +
(Part of Speech)

.... =
(Part of Speech)

MOVEMENT METER

How was your poop?

RATE YOUR POOP ON THE SCALE BELOW WITH A HAND-DRAWN POOP EMOJI:

 Dreadfully Dumpy

Positively Poo-tastic

TOILET PAPER SUPER BOWL

Choose your battle!

CIRCLE ONE:
* SOFTEST FEEL *   * CATCHIEST JINGLE *   * HARDEST WORKING *

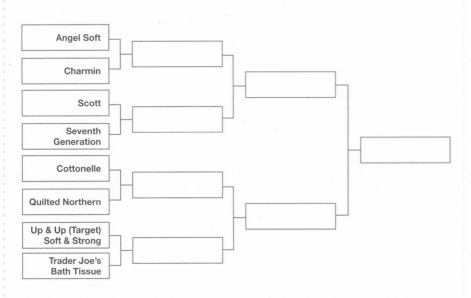

Angel Soft

Charmin

Scott

Seventh Generation

Cottonelle

Quilted Northern

Up & Up (Target) Soft & Strong

Trader Joe's Bath Tissue

.... , you're on a roll!

Winning Team

QUALITY ASS-URANCE

How did we doo-doo?

RATE YOUR EXPERIENCE ON A SCALE OF
1 TO 5, 5 MEANING EXTREMELY SATISFIED.

Cleanliness ☆ ☆ ☆ ☆ ☆

Aesthetics ☆ ☆ ☆ ☆ ☆

Toilet Paper ☆ ☆ ☆ ☆ ☆

Spray/SoapScent ☆ ☆ ☆ ☆ ☆

Privacy ☆ ☆ ☆ ☆ ☆

Ventilation ☆ ☆ ☆ ☆ ☆

Plunger Power ☆ ☆ ☆ ☆ ☆

THANKS FOR DROPPING BY

THANKS FOR DROPPING BY

YOUR NAME:

....

IF YOU'RE NOT HERE TO SEE A MAN ABOUT A HORSE, WHAT BROUGHT YOU TO THE LOO?

☐ Just a wiz, lay off!
☐ Freshening up my make-up
☐ Escaping the crowd
☐ Letting out a secret fart or two
☐ Taking a self-guided tour
☐ Signing this stinkin' book
☐ Making a pit stop (ahem, reapplying deodorant—don't be nosy)
☐ Other:

....

....

DOO DOO-DLE

Draw a cute poo!

CREATE AND NAME YOUR DREAM BATHROOM FRESHENER SCENT

.... +
(Part of Speech)

.... +
(Part of Speech)

.... =
(Part of Speech)

MOVEMENT METER

How was your poop?

RATE YOUR POOP ON THE SCALE BELOW WITH A HAND-DRAWN POOP EMOJI:

 Dreadfully Dumpy

Positively Poo-tastic

TOILET PAPER SUPER BOWL

Choose your battle!

CIRCLE ONE:
* SOFTEST FEEL *   * CATCHIEST JINGLE *   * HARDEST WORKING *

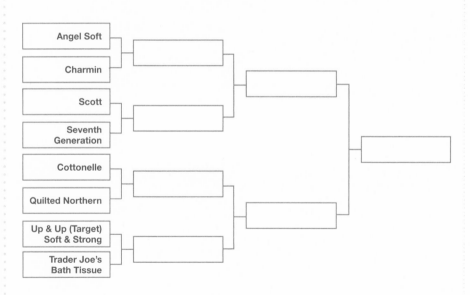

| Angel Soft |
| Charmin |
| Scott |
| Seventh Generation |
| Cottonelle |
| Quilted Northern |
| Up & Up (Target) Soft & Strong |
| Trader Joe's Bath Tissue |

.... , you're on a roll!

Winning Team

QUALITY ASS-URANCE

How did we doo-doo?

RATE YOUR EXPERIENCE ON A SCALE OF
1 TO 5, 5 MEANING EXTREMELY SATISFIED.

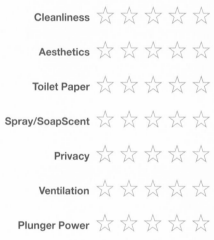

Cleanliness ☆ ☆ ☆ ☆ ☆

Aesthetics ☆ ☆ ☆ ☆ ☆

Toilet Paper ☆ ☆ ☆ ☆ ☆

Spray/SoapScent ☆ ☆ ☆ ☆ ☆

Privacy ☆ ☆ ☆ ☆ ☆

Ventilation ☆ ☆ ☆ ☆ ☆

Plunger Power ☆ ☆ ☆ ☆ ☆

THANKS FOR DROPPING BY

THANKS FOR DROPPING BY

YOUR NAME:

....

IF YOU'RE NOT HERE TO SEE A MAN ABOUT A HORSE, WHAT BROUGHT YOU TO THE LOO?

☐ Just a wiz, lay off!

☐ Freshening up my make-up

☐ Escaping the crowd

☐ Letting out a secret fart or two

☐ Taking a self-guided tour

☐ Signing this stinkin' book

☐ Making a pit stop (ahem, reapplying
   deodorant—don't be nosy)

☐ Other:

....

....

DOO DOO-DLE

Draw a cute poo!

**CREATE AND NAME YOUR DREAM
BATHROOM FRESHENER SCENT**

.... +
(Part of Speech)

.... +
(Part of Speech)

.... =
(Part of Speech)

MOVEMENT METER

How was your poop?

**RATE YOUR POOP ON THE SCALE BELOW
WITH A HAND-DRAWN POOP EMOJI:**

 Dreadfully Dumpy

Positively Poo-tastic

TOILET PAPER SUPER BOWL

Choose your battle!

CIRCLE ONE:
* SOFTEST FEEL *   * CATCHIEST JINGLE *   * HARDEST WORKING *

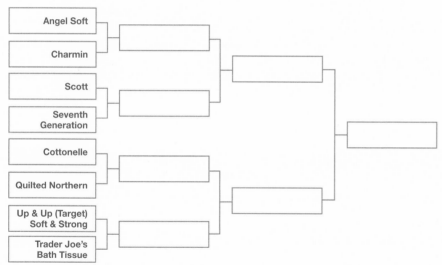

- Angel Soft
- Charmin
- Scott
- Seventh Generation
- Cottonelle
- Quilted Northern
- Up & Up (Target) Soft & Strong
- Trader Joe's Bath Tissue

.... , you're on a roll!

Winning Team

QUALITY ASS-URANCE

How did we doo-doo?

RATE YOUR EXPERIENCE ON A SCALE OF 1 TO 5, 5 MEANING EXTREMELY SATISFIED.

Cleanliness ☆ ☆ ☆ ☆ ☆

Aesthetics ☆ ☆ ☆ ☆ ☆

Toilet Paper ☆ ☆ ☆ ☆ ☆

Spray/SoapScent ☆ ☆ ☆ ☆ ☆

Privacy ☆ ☆ ☆ ☆ ☆

Ventilation ☆ ☆ ☆ ☆ ☆

Plunger Power ☆ ☆ ☆ ☆ ☆

THANKS FOR DROPPING BY

THANKS FOR DROPPING BY

YOUR NAME:

....

IF YOU'RE NOT HERE TO SEE A MAN ABOUT A HORSE, WHAT BROUGHT YOU TO THE LOO?

☐ Just a wiz, lay off!

☐ Freshening up my make-up

☐ Escaping the crowd

☐ Letting out a secret fart or two

☐ Taking a self-guided tour

☐ Signing this stinkin' book

☐ Making a pit stop (ahem, reapplying deodorant—don't be nosy)

☐ Other:

....

....

DOO DOO-DLE

Draw a cute poo!

CREATE AND NAME YOUR DREAM BATHROOM FRESHENER SCENT

.... +

(Part of Speech)

.... +

(Part of Speech)

.... =

(Part of Speech)

....

MOVEMENT METER

How was your poop?

RATE YOUR POOP ON THE SCALE BELOW WITH A HAND-DRAWN POOP EMOJI:

 Dreadfully Dumpy

 Positively Poo-tastic

TOILET PAPER SUPER BOWL

Choose your battle!

CIRCLE ONE:
* SOFTEST FEEL *   * CATCHIEST JINGLE *   * HARDEST WORKING *

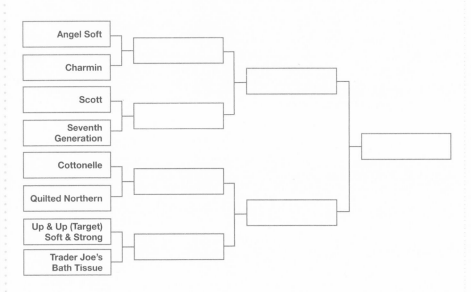

- Angel Soft
- Charmin
- Scott
- Seventh Generation
- Cottonelle
- Quilted Northern
- Up & Up (Target) Soft & Strong
- Trader Joe's Bath Tissue

.... , you're on a roll!

Winning Team

QUALITY ASS-URANCE

How did we doo-doo?

RATE YOUR EXPERIENCE ON A SCALE OF
1 TO 5, 5 MEANING EXTREMELY SATISFIED.

Cleanliness ☆ ☆ ☆ ☆ ☆

Aesthetics ☆ ☆ ☆ ☆ ☆

Toilet Paper ☆ ☆ ☆ ☆ ☆

Spray/SoapScent ☆ ☆ ☆ ☆ ☆

Privacy ☆ ☆ ☆ ☆ ☆

Ventilation ☆ ☆ ☆ ☆ ☆

Plunger Power ☆ ☆ ☆ ☆ ☆

THANKS FOR
DROPPING BY

THANKS FOR DROPPING BY

YOUR NAME:

....

IF YOU'RE NOT HERE TO SEE A MAN ABOUT A HORSE, WHAT BROUGHT YOU TO THE LOO?

☐ Just a wiz, lay off!

☐ Freshening up my make-up

☐ Escaping the crowd

☐ Letting out a secret fart or two

☐ Taking a self-guided tour

☐ Signing this stinkin' book

☐ Making a pit stop (ahem, reapplying deodorant—don't be nosy)

☐ Other:

....

....

DOO DOO-DLE

Draw a cute poo!

CREATE AND NAME YOUR DREAM BATHROOM FRESHENER SCENT

.... +

(Part of Speech)

.... +

(Part of Speech)

.... =

(Part of Speech)

MOVEMENT METER

How was your poop?

RATE YOUR POOP ON THE SCALE BELOW WITH A HAND-DRAWN POOP EMOJI:

 Dreadfully Dumpy

 Positively Poo-tastic

TOILET PAPER SUPER BOWL

Choose your battle!

CIRCLE ONE:
* SOFTEST FEEL *   * CATCHIEST JINGLE *   * HARDEST WORKING *

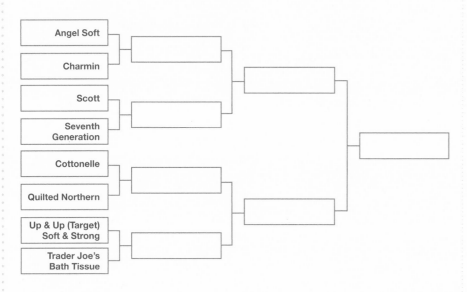

Angel Soft

Charmin

Scott

Seventh
Generation

Cottonelle

Quilted Northern

Up & Up (Target)
Soft & Strong

Trader Joe's
Bath Tissue

.... , you're on a roll!

Winning Team

QUALITY ASS-URANCE

How did we doo-doo?

RATE YOUR EXPERIENCE ON A SCALE OF
1 TO 5, 5 MEANING EXTREMELY SATISFIED.

Cleanliness ☆ ☆ ☆ ☆ ☆

Aesthetics ☆ ☆ ☆ ☆ ☆

Toilet Paper ☆ ☆ ☆ ☆ ☆

Spray/SoapScent ☆ ☆ ☆ ☆ ☆

Privacy ☆ ☆ ☆ ☆ ☆

Ventilation ☆ ☆ ☆ ☆ ☆

Plunger Power ☆ ☆ ☆ ☆ ☆

THANKS FOR
DROPPING BY

THANKS FOR DROPPING BY

YOUR NAME:

....

IF YOU'RE NOT HERE TO SEE A MAN ABOUT A HORSE, WHAT BROUGHT YOU TO THE LOO?

☐ Just a wiz, lay off!

☐ Freshening up my make-up

☐ Escaping the crowd

☐ Letting out a secret fart or two

☐ Taking a self-guided tour

☐ Signing this stinkin' book

☐ Making a pit stop (ahem, reapplying deodorant—don't be nosy)

☐ Other:

....

....

DOO DOO-DLE

Draw a cute poo!

CREATE AND NAME YOUR DREAM BATHROOM FRESHENER SCENT

.... +
(Part of Speech)

.... +
(Part of Speech)

.... =
(Part of Speech)

MOVEMENT METER

How was your poop?

RATE YOUR POOP ON THE SCALE BELOW WITH A HAND-DRAWN POOP EMOJI:

 Dreadfully Dumpy

Positively Poo-tastic

TOILET PAPER SUPER BOWL

Choose your battle!

CIRCLE ONE:
* SOFTEST FEEL *   * CATCHIEST JINGLE *   * HARDEST WORKING *

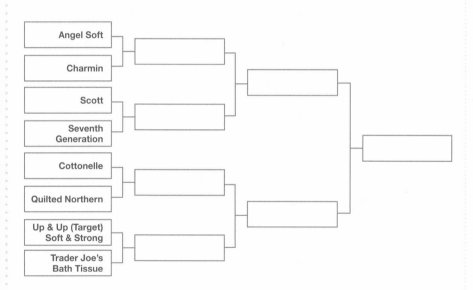

- Angel Soft
- Charmin
- Scott
- Seventh Generation
- Cottonelle
- Quilted Northern
- Up & Up (Target) Soft & Strong
- Trader Joe's Bath Tissue

...., you're on a roll!

Winning Team

QUALITY ASS-URANCE

How did we doo-doo?

RATE YOUR EXPERIENCE ON A SCALE OF
1 TO 5, 5 MEANING EXTREMELY SATISFIED.

Cleanliness ☆ ☆ ☆ ☆ ☆

Aesthetics ☆ ☆ ☆ ☆ ☆

Toilet Paper ☆ ☆ ☆ ☆ ☆

Spray/SoapScent ☆ ☆ ☆ ☆ ☆

Privacy ☆ ☆ ☆ ☆ ☆

Ventilation ☆ ☆ ☆ ☆ ☆

Plunger Power ☆ ☆ ☆ ☆ ☆

THANKS FOR DROPPING BY

THANKS FOR DROPPING BY

YOUR NAME:

....

IF YOU'RE NOT HERE TO SEE A MAN ABOUT A HORSE, WHAT BROUGHT YOU TO THE LOO?

☐ Just a wiz, lay off!
☐ Freshening up my make-up
☐ Escaping the crowd
☐ Letting out a secret fart or two
☐ Taking a self-guided tour
☐ Signing this stinkin' book
☐ Making a pit stop (ahem, reapplying deodorant—don't be nosy)
☐ Other:

....

....

DOO DOO-DLE

Draw a cute poo!

CREATE AND NAME YOUR DREAM BATHROOM FRESHENER SCENT

.... +
(Part of Speech)

.... +
(Part of Speech)

.... =
(Part of Speech)

MOVEMENT METER

How was your poop?

RATE YOUR POOP ON THE SCALE BELOW WITH A HAND-DRAWN POOP EMOJI:

 Dreadfully Dumpy

 **Positively Poo-tastic**

TOILET PAPER SUPER BOWL

Choose your battle!

CIRCLE ONE:
* SOFTEST FEEL * * CATCHIEST JINGLE * * HARDEST WORKING *

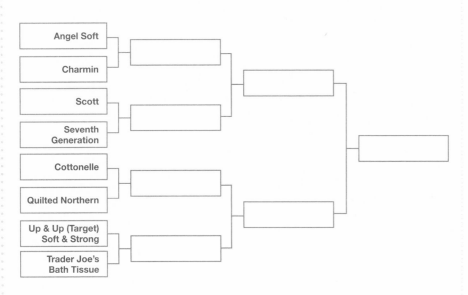

- Angel Soft
- Charmin
- Scott
- Seventh Generation
- Cottonelle
- Quilted Northern
- Up & Up (Target) Soft & Strong
- Trader Joe's Bath Tissue

...., you're on a roll!

Winning Team

QUALITY ASS-URANCE

How did we doo-doo?

RATE YOUR EXPERIENCE ON A SCALE OF 1 TO 5, 5 MEANING EXTREMELY SATISFIED.

Cleanliness ☆ ☆ ☆ ☆ ☆

Aesthetics ☆ ☆ ☆ ☆ ☆

Toilet Paper ☆ ☆ ☆ ☆ ☆

Spray/SoapScent ☆ ☆ ☆ ☆ ☆

Privacy ☆ ☆ ☆ ☆ ☆

Ventilation ☆ ☆ ☆ ☆ ☆

Plunger Power ☆ ☆ ☆ ☆ ☆

THANKS FOR DROPPING BY

THANKS FOR DROPPING BY

YOUR NAME:

....

IF YOU'RE NOT HERE TO SEE A MAN ABOUT A HORSE, WHAT BROUGHT YOU TO THE LOO?

☐ Just a wiz, lay off!
☐ Freshening up my make-up
☐ Escaping the crowd
☐ Letting out a secret fart or two
☐ Taking a self-guided tour
☐ Signing this stinkin' book
☐ Making a pit stop (ahem, reapplying deodorant—don't be nosy)
☐ Other:

....

....

DOO DOO-DLE

Draw a cute poo!

CREATE AND NAME YOUR DREAM BATHROOM FRESHENER SCENT

.... +
(Part of Speech)

.... +
(Part of Speech)

.... =
(Part of Speech)

MOVEMENT METER

How was your poop?

RATE YOUR POOP ON THE SCALE BELOW WITH A HAND-DRAWN POOP EMOJI:

 Dreadfully Dumpy

Positively Poo-tastic

TOILET PAPER SUPER BOWL

Choose your battle!

CIRCLE ONE:
* SOFTEST FEEL *   * CATCHIEST JINGLE *   * HARDEST WORKING *

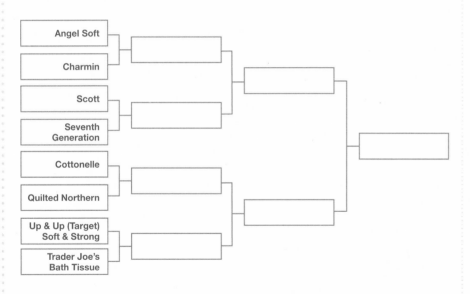

Angel Soft	
Charmin	
Scott	
Seventh Generation	
Cottonelle	
Quilted Northern	
Up & Up (Target) Soft & Strong	
Trader Joe's Bath Tissue	

.... , you're on a roll!

Winning Team

QUALITY ASS-URANCE

How did we doo-doo?

RATE YOUR EXPERIENCE ON A SCALE OF
1 TO 5, 5 MEANING EXTREMELY SATISFIED.

Cleanliness ☆ ☆ ☆ ☆ ☆

Aesthetics ☆ ☆ ☆ ☆ ☆

Toilet Paper ☆ ☆ ☆ ☆ ☆

Spray/SoapScent ☆ ☆ ☆ ☆ ☆

Privacy ☆ ☆ ☆ ☆ ☆

Ventilation ☆ ☆ ☆ ☆ ☆

Plunger Power ☆ ☆ ☆ ☆ ☆

THANKS FOR DROPPING BY

THANKS FOR DROPPING BY

YOUR NAME:

....

IF YOU'RE NOT HERE TO SEE A MAN ABOUT A HORSE, WHAT BROUGHT YOU TO THE LOO?

☐ Just a wiz, lay off!
☐ Freshening up my make-up
☐ Escaping the crowd
☐ Letting out a secret fart or two
☐ Taking a self-guided tour
☐ Signing this stinkin' book
☐ Making a pit stop (ahem, reapplying deodorant—don't be nosy)
☐ Other:

....

DOO DOO-DLE

Draw a cute poo!

CREATE AND NAME YOUR DREAM BATHROOM FRESHENER SCENT

.... +
(Part of Speech)

.... +
(Part of Speech)

.... =
(Part of Speech)

MOVEMENT METER

How was your poop?

RATE YOUR POOP ON THE SCALE BELOW WITH A HAND-DRAWN POOP EMOJI:

 Dreadfully Dumpy

Positively Poo-tastic

TOILET PAPER SUPER BOWL

Choose your battle!

CIRCLE ONE:
* SOFTEST FEEL *   * CATCHIEST JINGLE *   * HARDEST WORKING *

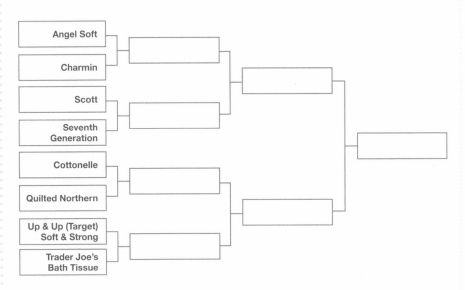

Angel Soft

Charmin

Scott

Seventh Generation

Cottonelle

Quilted Northern

Up & Up (Target) Soft & Strong

Trader Joe's Bath Tissue

.... , you're on a roll!

Winning Team

QUALITY ASS-URANCE

How did we doo-doo?

RATE YOUR EXPERIENCE ON A SCALE OF 1 TO 5, 5 MEANING EXTREMELY SATISFIED.

Cleanliness ☆ ☆ ☆ ☆ ☆

Aesthetics ☆ ☆ ☆ ☆ ☆

Toilet Paper ☆ ☆ ☆ ☆ ☆

Spray/Soap Scent ☆ ☆ ☆ ☆ ☆

Privacy ☆ ☆ ☆ ☆ ☆

Ventilation ☆ ☆ ☆ ☆ ☆

Plunger Power ☆ ☆ ☆ ☆ ☆

THANKS FOR DROPPING BY

THANKS FOR DROPPING BY

YOUR NAME:

....

IF YOU'RE NOT HERE TO SEE A MAN ABOUT A HORSE, WHAT BROUGHT YOU TO THE LOO?

☐ Just a wiz, lay off!
☐ Freshening up my make-up
☐ Escaping the crowd
☐ Letting out a secret fart or two
☐ Taking a self-guided tour
☐ Signing this stinkin' book
☐ Making a pit stop (ahem, reapplying deodorant—don't be nosy)
☐ Other:

....

DOO DOO-DLE

Draw a cute poo!

CREATE AND NAME YOUR DREAM BATHROOM FRESHENER SCENT

.... +
(Part of Speech)

.... +
(Part of Speech)

.... =
(Part of Speech)

MOVEMENT METER

How was your poop?

RATE YOUR POOP ON THE SCALE BELOW WITH A HAND-DRAWN POOP EMOJI:

 Dreadfully Dumpy

 Positively Poo-tastic

TOILET PAPER SUPER BOWL

Choose your battle!

CIRCLE ONE:
* SOFTEST FEEL *   * CATCHIEST JINGLE *   * HARDEST WORKING *

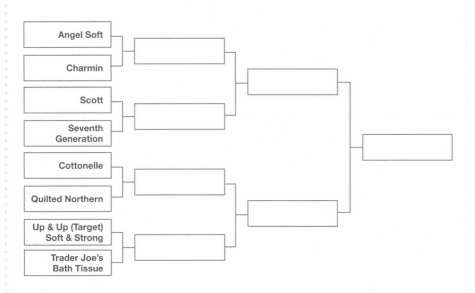

Angel Soft

Charmin

Scott

Seventh Generation

Cottonelle

Quilted Northern

Up & Up (Target) Soft & Strong

Trader Joe's Bath Tissue

...., you're on a roll!

Winning Team

QUALITY ASS-URANCE

How did we doo-doo?

RATE YOUR EXPERIENCE ON A SCALE OF
1 TO 5, 5 MEANING EXTREMELY SATISFIED.

Cleanliness ☆ ☆ ☆ ☆ ☆

Aesthetics ☆ ☆ ☆ ☆ ☆

Toilet Paper ☆ ☆ ☆ ☆ ☆

Spray/SoapScent ☆ ☆ ☆ ☆ ☆

Privacy ☆ ☆ ☆ ☆ ☆

Ventilation ☆ ☆ ☆ ☆ ☆

Plunger Power ☆ ☆ ☆ ☆ ☆

THANKS FOR DROPPING BY

THANKS FOR DROPPING BY

YOUR NAME:

....

**IF YOU'RE NOT HERE TO SEE A MAN ABOUT
A HORSE, WHAT BROUGHT YOU TO THE LOO?**

☐ Just a wiz, lay off!

☐ Freshening up my make-up

☐ Escaping the crowd

☐ Letting out a secret fart or two

☐ Taking a self-guided tour

☐ Signing this stinkin' book

☐ Making a pit stop (ahem, reapplying
   deodorant—don't be nosy)

☐ Other:

....

DOO DOO-DLE

Draw a cute poo!

**CREATE AND NAME YOUR DREAM
BATHROOM FRESHENER SCENT**

.... +

(Part of Speech)

.... +

(Part of Speech)

.... =

(Part of Speech)

MOVEMENT METER

How was your poop?

**RATE YOUR POOP ON THE SCALE BELOW
WITH A HAND-DRAWN POOP EMOJI:**

 Dreadfully Dumpy

Positively Poo-tastic

TOILET PAPER SUPER BOWL

Choose your battle!

CIRCLE ONE:
* SOFTEST FEEL *   * CATCHIEST JINGLE *   * HARDEST WORKING *

Angel Soft

Charmin

Scott

Seventh Generation

Cottonelle

Quilted Northern

Up & Up (Target) Soft & Strong

Trader Joe's Bath Tissue

...., you're on a roll!

Winning Team

QUALITY ASS-URANCE

How did we doo-doo?

RATE YOUR EXPERIENCE ON A SCALE OF
1 TO 5, 5 MEANING EXTREMELY SATISFIED.

Cleanliness ☆ ☆ ☆ ☆ ☆

Aesthetics ☆ ☆ ☆ ☆ ☆

Toilet Paper ☆ ☆ ☆ ☆ ☆

Spray/SoapScent ☆ ☆ ☆ ☆ ☆

Privacy ☆ ☆ ☆ ☆ ☆

Ventilation ☆ ☆ ☆ ☆ ☆

Plunger Power ☆ ☆ ☆ ☆ ☆

THANKS FOR DROPPING BY

THANKS FOR DROPPING BY

YOUR NAME:

....

IF YOU'RE NOT HERE TO SEE A MAN ABOUT A HORSE, WHAT BROUGHT YOU TO THE LOO?

- ☐ Just a wiz, lay off!
- ☐ Freshening up my make-up
- ☐ Escaping the crowd
- ☐ Letting out a secret fart or two
- ☐ Taking a self-guided tour
- ☐ Signing this stinkin' book
- ☐ Making a pit stop (ahem, reapplying deodorant—don't be nosy)
- ☐ Other:

....

DOO DOO-DLE

Draw a cute poo!

CREATE AND NAME YOUR DREAM BATHROOM FRESHENER SCENT

.... +
(Part of Speech)

.... +
(Part of Speech)

.... =
(Part of Speech)

....

MOVEMENT METER

How was your poop?

RATE YOUR POOP ON THE SCALE BELOW WITH A HAND-DRAWN POOP EMOJI:

 Dreadfully Dumpy

 Positively Poo-tastic

TOILET PAPER SUPER BOWL

Choose your battle!

CIRCLE ONE:
* SOFTEST FEEL *   * CATCHIEST JINGLE *   * HARDEST WORKING *

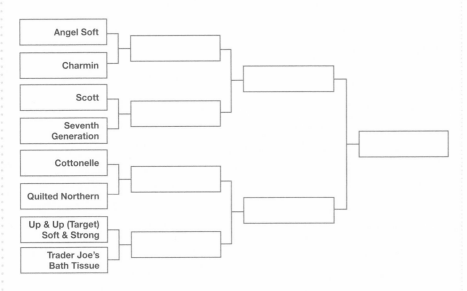

Angel Soft

Charmin

Scott

Seventh Generation

Cottonelle

Quilted Northern

Up & Up (Target) Soft & Strong

Trader Joe's Bath Tissue

.... , you're on a roll!

Winning Team

QUALITY ASS-URANCE

How did we doo-doo?

RATE YOUR EXPERIENCE ON A SCALE OF 1 TO 5, 5 MEANING EXTREMELY SATISFIED.

Cleanliness ☆ ☆ ☆ ☆ ☆

Aesthetics ☆ ☆ ☆ ☆ ☆

Toilet Paper ☆ ☆ ☆ ☆ ☆

Spray/SoapScent ☆ ☆ ☆ ☆ ☆

Privacy ☆ ☆ ☆ ☆ ☆

Ventilation ☆ ☆ ☆ ☆ ☆

Plunger Power ☆ ☆ ☆ ☆ ☆

THANKS FOR DROPPING BY

THANKS FOR DROPPING BY

YOUR NAME:

....

IF YOU'RE NOT HERE TO SEE A MAN ABOUT
A HORSE, WHAT BROUGHT YOU TO THE LOO?

☐ Just a wiz, lay off!
☐ Freshening up my make-up
☐ Escaping the crowd
☐ Letting out a secret fart or two
☐ Taking a self-guided tour
☐ Signing this stinkin' book
☐ Making a pit stop (ahem, reapplying
   deodorant—don't be nosy)
☐ Other:

....

....

DOO DOO-DLE

Draw a cute poo!

CREATE AND NAME YOUR DREAM
BATHROOM FRESHENER SCENT

.... +
(Part of Speech)

.... +
(Part of Speech)

.... =
(Part of Speech)

....

MOVEMENT METER

How was your poop?

RATE YOUR POOP ON THE SCALE BELOW
WITH A HAND-DRAWN POOP EMOJI:

 Dreadfully Dumpy

 Positively Poo-tastic

TOILET PAPER SUPER BOWL

Choose your battle!

CIRCLE ONE:
* SOFTEST FEEL *   * CATCHIEST JINGLE *   * HARDEST WORKING *

Angel Soft	
Charmin	
Scott	
Seventh Generation	
Cottonelle	
Quilted Northern	
Up & Up (Target) Soft & Strong	
Trader Joe's Bath Tissue	

.... , you're on a roll!

Winning Team

QUALITY ASS-URANCE

How did we doo-doo?

RATE YOUR EXPERIENCE ON A SCALE OF 1 TO 5, 5 MEANING EXTREMELY SATISFIED.

Cleanliness ☆ ☆ ☆ ☆ ☆

Aesthetics ☆ ☆ ☆ ☆ ☆

Toilet Paper ☆ ☆ ☆ ☆ ☆

Spray/SoapScent ☆ ☆ ☆ ☆ ☆

Privacy ☆ ☆ ☆ ☆ ☆

Ventilation ☆ ☆ ☆ ☆ ☆

Plunger Power ☆ ☆ ☆ ☆ ☆

THANKS FOR DROPPING BY

THANKS FOR DROPPING BY

YOUR NAME:

....

IF YOU'RE NOT HERE TO SEE A MAN ABOUT A HORSE, WHAT BROUGHT YOU TO THE LOO?

☐ Just a wiz, lay off!
☐ Freshening up my make-up
☐ Escaping the crowd
☐ Letting out a secret fart or two
☐ Taking a self-guided tour
☐ Signing this stinkin' book
☐ Making a pit stop (ahem, reapplying deodorant—don't be nosy)
☐ Other:

....

DOO DOO-DLE

Draw a cute poo!

CREATE AND NAME YOUR DREAM BATHROOM FRESHENER SCENT

.... +
(Part of Speech)

.... +
(Part of Speech)

.... =
(Part of Speech)

....

MOVEMENT METER

How was your poop?

RATE YOUR POOP ON THE SCALE BELOW WITH A HAND-DRAWN POOP EMOJI:

 Dreadfully Dumpy

Positively Poo-tastic

TOILET PAPER SUPER BOWL

Choose your battle!

CIRCLE ONE:
* SOFTEST FEEL *   * CATCHIEST JINGLE *   * HARDEST WORKING *

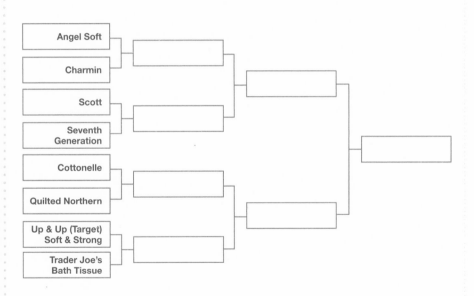

Angel Soft

Charmin

Scott

Seventh Generation

Cottonelle

Quilted Northern

Up & Up (Target) Soft & Strong

Trader Joe's Bath Tissue

...., you're on a roll!

Winning Team

QUALITY ASS-URANCE

How did we doo-doo?

RATE YOUR EXPERIENCE ON A SCALE OF
1 TO 5, 5 MEANING EXTREMELY SATISFIED.

Cleanliness ☆ ☆ ☆ ☆ ☆

Aesthetics ☆ ☆ ☆ ☆ ☆

Toilet Paper ☆ ☆ ☆ ☆ ☆

Spray/SoapScent ☆ ☆ ☆ ☆ ☆

Privacy ☆ ☆ ☆ ☆ ☆

Ventilation ☆ ☆ ☆ ☆ ☆

Plunger Power ☆ ☆ ☆ ☆ ☆

THANKS FOR DROPPING BY

THANKS FOR DROPPING BY

YOUR NAME:

....

IF YOU'RE NOT HERE TO SEE A MAN ABOUT A HORSE, WHAT BROUGHT YOU TO THE LOO?

☐ Just a wiz, lay off!
☐ Freshening up my make-up
☐ Escaping the crowd
☐ Letting out a secret fart or two
☐ Taking a self-guided tour
☐ Signing this stinkin' book
☐ Making a pit stop (ahem, reapplying
   deodorant—don't be nosy)
☐ Other:

....

....

DOO DOO-DLE

Draw a cute poo!

CREATE AND NAME YOUR DREAM BATHROOM FRESHENER SCENT

.... +
(Part of Speech)

.... +
(Part of Speech)

.... =
(Part of Speech)

MOVEMENT METER

How was your poop?

RATE YOUR POOP ON THE SCALE BELOW WITH A HAND-DRAWN POOP EMOJI:

 Dreadfully Dumpy

 Positively Poo-tastic

TOILET PAPER SUPER BOWL

Choose your battle!

CIRCLE ONE:
* SOFTEST FEEL *   * CATCHIEST JINGLE *   * HARDEST WORKING *

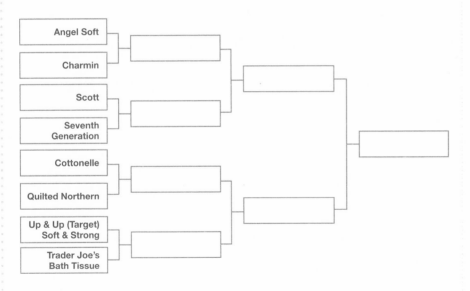

...., you're on a roll!

Winning Team

QUALITY ASS-URANCE

How did we doo-doo?

RATE YOUR EXPERIENCE ON A SCALE OF 1 TO 5, 5 MEANING EXTREMELY SATISFIED.

Cleanliness ☆ ☆ ☆ ☆ ☆

Aesthetics ☆ ☆ ☆ ☆ ☆

Toilet Paper ☆ ☆ ☆ ☆ ☆

Spray/SoapScent ☆ ☆ ☆ ☆ ☆

Privacy ☆ ☆ ☆ ☆ ☆

Ventilation ☆ ☆ ☆ ☆ ☆

Plunger Power ☆ ☆ ☆ ☆ ☆

THANKS FOR DROPPING BY

THANKS FOR DROPPING BY

YOUR NAME:

....

IF YOU'RE NOT HERE TO SEE A MAN ABOUT A HORSE, WHAT BROUGHT YOU TO THE LOO?

☐ Just a wiz, lay off!

☐ Freshening up my make-up

☐ Escaping the crowd

☐ Letting out a secret fart or two

☐ Taking a self-guided tour

☐ Signing this stinkin' book

☐ Making a pit stop (ahem, reapplying deodorant—don't be nosy)

☐ Other:

....

DOO DOO-DLE

Draw a cute poo!

CREATE AND NAME YOUR DREAM BATHROOM FRESHENER SCENT

.... +

(Part of Speech)

.... +

(Part of Speech)

.... =

(Part of Speech)

MOVEMENT METER

How was your poop?

RATE YOUR POOP ON THE SCALE BELOW WITH A HAND-DRAWN POOP EMOJI:

 Dreadfully Dumpy

 **Positively Poo-tastic**

TOILET PAPER SUPER BOWL

Choose your battle!

CIRCLE ONE:
* SOFTEST FEEL *   * CATCHIEST JINGLE *   * HARDEST WORKING *

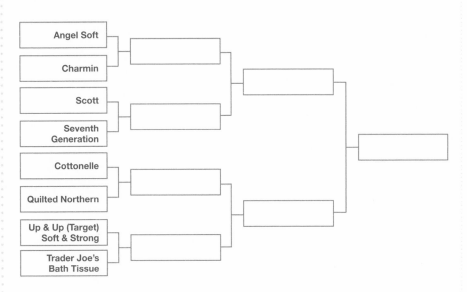

- Angel Soft
- Charmin
- Scott
- Seventh Generation
- Cottonelle
- Quilted Northern
- Up & Up (Target) Soft & Strong
- Trader Joe's Bath Tissue

...., you're on a roll!

Winning Team

QUALITY ASS-URANCE

How did we doo-doo?

RATE YOUR EXPERIENCE ON A SCALE OF 1 TO 5, 5 MEANING EXTREMELY SATISFIED.

Cleanliness ☆ ☆ ☆ ☆ ☆

Aesthetics ☆ ☆ ☆ ☆ ☆

Toilet Paper ☆ ☆ ☆ ☆ ☆

Spray/SoapScent ☆ ☆ ☆ ☆ ☆

Privacy ☆ ☆ ☆ ☆ ☆

Ventilation ☆ ☆ ☆ ☆ ☆

Plunger Power ☆ ☆ ☆ ☆ ☆

THANKS FOR DROPPING BY

THANKS FOR DROPPING BY

YOUR NAME:

....

IF YOU'RE NOT HERE TO SEE A MAN ABOUT A HORSE, WHAT BROUGHT YOU TO THE LOO?

☐ Just a wiz, lay off!
☐ Freshening up my make-up
☐ Escaping the crowd
☐ Letting out a secret fart or two
☐ Taking a self-guided tour
☐ Signing this stinkin' book
☐ Making a pit stop (ahem, reapplying deodorant—don't be nosy)
☐ Other:

....

DOO DOO-DLE

Draw a cute poo!

CREATE AND NAME YOUR DREAM BATHROOM FRESHENER SCENT

.... +
(Part of Speech)

.... +
(Part of Speech)

.... =
(Part of Speech)

MOVEMENT METER

How was your poop?

RATE YOUR POOP ON THE SCALE BELOW WITH A HAND-DRAWN POOP EMOJI:

 Dreadfully Dumpy

Positively Poo-tastic

TOILET PAPER SUPER BOWL

Choose your battle!

CIRCLE ONE:
* SOFTEST FEEL *   * CATCHIEST JINGLE *   * HARDEST WORKING *

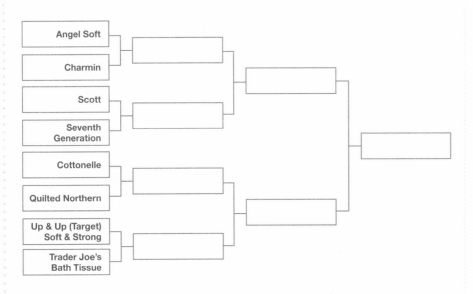

- Angel Soft
- Charmin
- Scott
- Seventh Generation
- Cottonelle
- Quilted Northern
- Up & Up (Target) Soft & Strong
- Trader Joe's Bath Tissue

...., you're on a roll!

Winning Team

QUALITY ASS-URANCE

How did we doo-doo?

RATE YOUR EXPERIENCE ON A SCALE OF
1 TO 5, 5 MEANING EXTREMELY SATISFIED.

Cleanliness ☆ ☆ ☆ ☆ ☆

Aesthetics ☆ ☆ ☆ ☆ ☆

Toilet Paper ☆ ☆ ☆ ☆ ☆

Spray/SoapScent ☆ ☆ ☆ ☆ ☆

Privacy ☆ ☆ ☆ ☆ ☆

Ventilation ☆ ☆ ☆ ☆ ☆

Plunger Power ☆ ☆ ☆ ☆ ☆

THANKS FOR DROPPING BY

THANKS FOR DROPPING BY

YOUR NAME:

....

IF YOU'RE NOT HERE TO SEE A MAN ABOUT A HORSE, WHAT BROUGHT YOU TO THE LOO?

☐ Just a wiz, lay off!
☐ Freshening up my make-up
☐ Escaping the crowd
☐ Letting out a secret fart or two
☐ Taking a self-guided tour
☐ Signing this stinkin' book
☐ Making a pit stop (ahem, reapplying deodorant—don't be nosy)
☐ Other:

....

....

DOO DOO-DLE

Draw a cute poo!

CREATE AND NAME YOUR DREAM BATHROOM FRESHENER SCENT

....   +
(Part of Speech)

....   +
(Part of Speech)

....   =
(Part of Speech)

MOVEMENT METER

How was your poop?

RATE YOUR POOP ON THE SCALE BELOW WITH A HAND-DRAWN POOP EMOJI:

 Dreadfully Dumpy

 Positively Poo-tastic

TOILET PAPER SUPER BOWL

Choose your battle!

CIRCLE ONE:
* SOFTEST FEEL *   * CATCHIEST JINGLE *   * HARDEST WORKING *

Angel Soft

Charmin

Scott

Seventh Generation

Cottonelle

Quilted Northern

Up & Up (Target) Soft & Strong

Trader Joe's Bath Tissue

.... , you're on a roll!

Winning Team

QUALITY ASS-URANCE

How did we doo-doo?

RATE YOUR EXPERIENCE ON A SCALE OF 1 TO 5, 5 MEANING EXTREMELY SATISFIED.

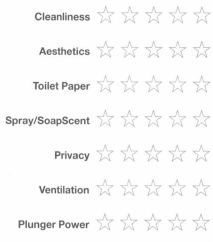

Cleanliness ☆ ☆ ☆ ☆ ☆

Aesthetics ☆ ☆ ☆ ☆ ☆

Toilet Paper ☆ ☆ ☆ ☆ ☆

Spray/SoapScent ☆ ☆ ☆ ☆ ☆

Privacy ☆ ☆ ☆ ☆ ☆

Ventilation ☆ ☆ ☆ ☆ ☆

Plunger Power ☆ ☆ ☆ ☆ ☆

THANKS FOR DROPPING BY

THANKS FOR DROPPING BY

YOUR NAME:

....

IF YOU'RE NOT HERE TO SEE A MAN ABOUT A HORSE, WHAT BROUGHT YOU TO THE LOO?

☐ Just a wiz, lay off!
☐ Freshening up my make-up
☐ Escaping the crowd
☐ Letting out a secret fart or two
☐ Taking a self-guided tour
☐ Signing this stinkin' book
☐ Making a pit stop (ahem, reapplying
    deodorant—don't be nosy)
☐ Other:

....

DOO DOO-DLE

Draw a cute poo!

**CREATE AND NAME YOUR DREAM
BATHROOM FRESHENER SCENT**

.... +
(Part of Speech)

.... +
(Part of Speech)

.... =
(Part of Speech)

....

MOVEMENT METER

How was your poop?

**RATE YOUR POOP ON THE SCALE BELOW
WITH A HAND-DRAWN POOP EMOJI:**

 Dreadfully Dumpy

 **Positively Poo-tastic**

TOILET PAPER SUPER BOWL

Choose your battle!

CIRCLE ONE:
* SOFTEST FEEL * * CATCHIEST JINGLE * * HARDEST WORKING *

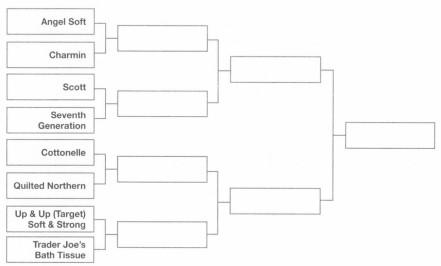

Angel Soft

Charmin

Scott

Seventh Generation

Cottonelle

Quilted Northern

Up & Up (Target) Soft & Strong

Trader Joe's Bath Tissue

.... , you're on a roll!

Winning Team

QUALITY ASS-URANCE

How did we doo-doo?

RATE YOUR EXPERIENCE ON A SCALE OF 1 TO 5, 5 MEANING EXTREMELY SATISFIED.

Cleanliness ☆ ☆ ☆ ☆ ☆

Aesthetics ☆ ☆ ☆ ☆ ☆

Toilet Paper ☆ ☆ ☆ ☆ ☆

Spray/SoapScent ☆ ☆ ☆ ☆ ☆

Privacy ☆ ☆ ☆ ☆ ☆

Ventilation ☆ ☆ ☆ ☆ ☆

Plunger Power ☆ ☆ ☆ ☆ ☆

THANKS FOR DROPPING BY

THANKS FOR DROPPING BY

YOUR NAME:

....

IF YOU'RE NOT HERE TO SEE A MAN ABOUT A HORSE, WHAT BROUGHT YOU TO THE LOO?

☐ Just a wiz, lay off!
☐ Freshening up my make-up
☐ Escaping the crowd
☐ Letting out a secret fart or two
☐ Taking a self-guided tour
☐ Signing this stinkin' book
☐ Making a pit stop (ahem, reapplying deodorant—don't be nosy)
☐ Other:

....

....

DOO DOO-DLE

Draw a cute poo!

CREATE AND NAME YOUR DREAM BATHROOM FRESHENER SCENT

.... +
(Part of Speech)

.... +
(Part of Speech)

.... =
(Part of Speech)

MOVEMENT METER

How was your poop?

RATE YOUR POOP ON THE SCALE BELOW WITH A HAND-DRAWN POOP EMOJI:

 Dreadfully Dumpy

Positively Poo-tastic

TOILET PAPER SUPER BOWL

Choose your battle!

CIRCLE ONE:
* SOFTEST FEEL *   * CATCHIEST JINGLE *   * HARDEST WORKING *

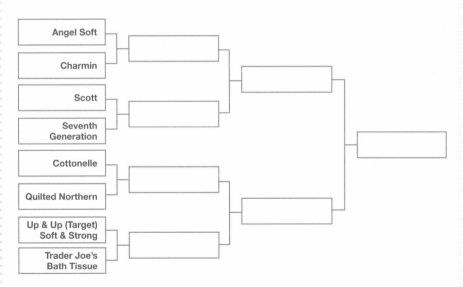

Angel Soft

Charmin

Scott

Seventh Generation

Cottonelle

Quilted Northern

Up & Up (Target) Soft & Strong

Trader Joe's Bath Tissue

...., you're on a roll!

Winning Team

QUALITY ASS-URANCE

How did we doo-doo?

RATE YOUR EXPERIENCE ON A SCALE OF 1 TO 5, 5 MEANING EXTREMELY SATISFIED.

Cleanliness ☆ ☆ ☆ ☆ ☆

Aesthetics ☆ ☆ ☆ ☆ ☆

Toilet Paper ☆ ☆ ☆ ☆ ☆

Spray/SoapScent ☆ ☆ ☆ ☆ ☆

Privacy ☆ ☆ ☆ ☆ ☆

Ventilation ☆ ☆ ☆ ☆ ☆

Plunger Power ☆ ☆ ☆ ☆ ☆

THANKS FOR DROPPING BY

THANKS FOR DROPPING BY

YOUR NAME:

....

IF YOU'RE NOT HERE TO SEE A MAN ABOUT A HORSE, WHAT BROUGHT YOU TO THE LOO?

☐ Just a wiz, lay off!

☐ Freshening up my make-up

☐ Escaping the crowd

☐ Letting out a secret fart or two

☐ Taking a self-guided tour

☐ Signing this stinkin' book

☐ Making a pit stop (ahem, reapplying deodorant—don't be nosy)

☐ Other:

....

....

DOO DOO-DLE

Draw a cute poo!

CREATE AND NAME YOUR DREAM BATHROOM FRESHENER SCENT

.... +
(Part of Speech)

.... +
(Part of Speech)

.... =
(Part of Speech)

MOVEMENT METER

How was your poop?

RATE YOUR POOP ON THE SCALE BELOW WITH A HAND-DRAWN POOP EMOJI:

 Dreadfully Dumpy

 Positively Poo-tastic

TOILET PAPER SUPER BOWL

Choose your battle!

CIRCLE ONE:
* SOFTEST FEEL *   * CATCHIEST JINGLE *   * HARDEST WORKING *

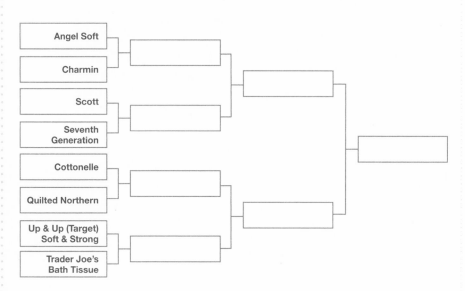

Angel Soft

Charmin

Scott

Seventh Generation

Cottonelle

Quilted Northern

Up & Up (Target) Soft & Strong

Trader Joe's Bath Tissue

...., you're on a roll!

Winning Team

QUALITY ASS-URANCE

How did we doo-doo?

RATE YOUR EXPERIENCE ON A SCALE OF 1 TO 5, 5 MEANING EXTREMELY SATISFIED.

Cleanliness ☆ ☆ ☆ ☆ ☆

Aesthetics ☆ ☆ ☆ ☆ ☆

Toilet Paper ☆ ☆ ☆ ☆ ☆

Spray/SoapScent ☆ ☆ ☆ ☆ ☆

Privacy ☆ ☆ ☆ ☆ ☆

Ventilation ☆ ☆ ☆ ☆ ☆

Plunger Power ☆ ☆ ☆ ☆ ☆

THANKS FOR DROPPING BY

THANKS FOR DROPPING BY

YOUR NAME:

....

IF YOU'RE NOT HERE TO SEE A MAN ABOUT A HORSE, WHAT BROUGHT YOU TO THE LOO?

☐ Just a wiz, lay off!
☐ Freshening up my make-up
☐ Escaping the crowd
☐ Letting out a secret fart or two
☐ Taking a self-guided tour
☐ Signing this stinkin' book
☐ Making a pit stop (ahem, reapplying
   deodorant—don't be nosy)
☐ Other:

....

....

DOO DOO-DLE

Draw a cute poo!

CREATE AND NAME YOUR DREAM BATHROOM FRESHENER SCENT

.... +
(Part of Speech)

.... +
(Part of Speech)

.... =
(Part of Speech)

MOVEMENT METER

How was your poop?

RATE YOUR POOP ON THE SCALE BELOW WITH A HAND-DRAWN POOP EMOJI:

 Dreadfully Dumpy

Positively Poo-tastic

TOILET PAPER SUPER BOWL

Choose your battle!

CIRCLE ONE:
* SOFTEST FEEL *   * CATCHIEST JINGLE *   * HARDEST WORKING *

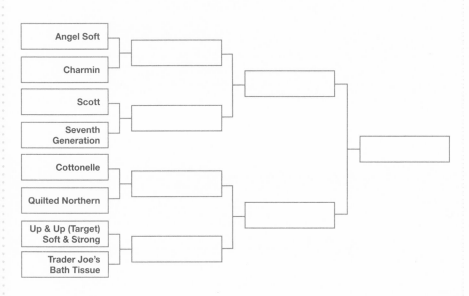

Angel Soft

Charmin

Scott

Seventh Generation

Cottonelle

Quilted Northern

Up & Up (Target) Soft & Strong

Trader Joe's Bath Tissue

.... , you're on a roll!

Winning Team

QUALITY ASS-URANCE

How did we doo-doo?

RATE YOUR EXPERIENCE ON A SCALE OF 1 TO 5, 5 MEANING EXTREMELY SATISFIED.

Cleanliness ☆ ☆ ☆ ☆ ☆

Aesthetics ☆ ☆ ☆ ☆ ☆

Toilet Paper ☆ ☆ ☆ ☆ ☆

Spray/SoapScent ☆ ☆ ☆ ☆ ☆

Privacy ☆ ☆ ☆ ☆ ☆

Ventilation ☆ ☆ ☆ ☆ ☆

Plunger Power ☆ ☆ ☆ ☆ ☆

THANKS FOR DROPPING BY

THANKS FOR DROPPING BY

YOUR NAME:

....

IF YOU'RE NOT HERE TO SEE A MAN ABOUT A HORSE, WHAT BROUGHT YOU TO THE LOO?

☐ Just a wiz, lay off!
☐ Freshening up my make-up
☐ Escaping the crowd
☐ Letting out a secret fart or two
☐ Taking a self-guided tour
☐ Signing this stinkin' book
☐ Making a pit stop (ahem, reapplying deodorant—don't be nosy)
☐ Other:

....

DOO DOO-DLE

Draw a cute poo!

CREATE AND NAME YOUR DREAM BATHROOM FRESHENER SCENT

.... **+**
(Part of Speech)

.... **+**
(Part of Speech)

.... **=**
(Part of Speech)

....

MOVEMENT METER

How was your poop?

RATE YOUR POOP ON THE SCALE BELOW WITH A HAND-DRAWN POOP EMOJI:

 Dreadfully Dumpy

Positively Poo-tastic

TOILET PAPER SUPER BOWL

Choose your battle!

CIRCLE ONE:
* SOFTEST FEEL *   * CATCHIEST JINGLE *   * HARDEST WORKING *

Angel Soft

Charmin

Scott

Seventh Generation

Cottonelle

Quilted Northern

Up & Up (Target) Soft & Strong

Trader Joe's Bath Tissue

...., you're on a roll!

Winning Team

QUALITY ASS-URANCE

How did we doo-doo?

RATE YOUR EXPERIENCE ON A SCALE OF 1 TO 5, 5 MEANING EXTREMELY SATISFIED.

Cleanliness ☆ ☆ ☆ ☆ ☆

Aesthetics ☆ ☆ ☆ ☆ ☆

Toilet Paper ☆ ☆ ☆ ☆ ☆

Spray/SoapScent ☆ ☆ ☆ ☆ ☆

Privacy ☆ ☆ ☆ ☆ ☆

Ventilation ☆ ☆ ☆ ☆ ☆

Plunger Power ☆ ☆ ☆ ☆ ☆

THANKS FOR DROPPING BY

THANKS FOR DROPPING BY

YOUR NAME:

....

IF YOU'RE NOT HERE TO SEE A MAN ABOUT A HORSE, WHAT BROUGHT YOU TO THE LOO?

☐ Just a wiz, lay off!
☐ Freshening up my make-up
☐ Escaping the crowd
☐ Letting out a secret fart or two
☐ Taking a self-guided tour
☐ Signing this stinkin' book
☐ Making a pit stop (ahem, reapplying deodorant—don't be nosy)
☐ Other:

....

....

DOO DOO-DLE

Draw a cute poo!

CREATE AND NAME YOUR DREAM BATHROOM FRESHENER SCENT

.... +
(Part of Speech)

.... +
(Part of Speech)

.... =
(Part of Speech)

....

MOVEMENT METER

How was your poop?

RATE YOUR POOP ON THE SCALE BELOW WITH A HAND-DRAWN POOP EMOJI:

 Dreadfully Dumpy

Positively Poo-tastic

TOILET PAPER SUPER BOWL

Choose your battle!

CIRCLE ONE:
* SOFTEST FEEL *   * CATCHIEST JINGLE *   * HARDEST WORKING *

Angel Soft

Charmin

Scott

Seventh Generation

Cottonelle

Quilted Northern

Up & Up (Target) Soft & Strong

Trader Joe's Bath Tissue

.... , you're on a roll!

Winning Team

QUALITY ASS-URANCE

How did we doo-doo?

RATE YOUR EXPERIENCE ON A SCALE OF
1 TO 5, 5 MEANING EXTREMELY SATISFIED.

Cleanliness ☆ ☆ ☆ ☆ ☆

Aesthetics ☆ ☆ ☆ ☆ ☆

Toilet Paper ☆ ☆ ☆ ☆ ☆

Spray/SoapScent ☆ ☆ ☆ ☆ ☆

Privacy ☆ ☆ ☆ ☆ ☆

Ventilation ☆ ☆ ☆ ☆ ☆

Plunger Power ☆ ☆ ☆ ☆ ☆

THANKS FOR DROPPING BY

THANKS FOR DROPPING BY

YOUR NAME:

....

IF YOU'RE NOT HERE TO SEE A MAN ABOUT A HORSE, WHAT BROUGHT YOU TO THE LOO?

☐ Just a wiz, lay off!

☐ Freshening up my make-up

☐ Escaping the crowd

☐ Letting out a secret fart or two

☐ Taking a self-guided tour

☐ Signing this stinkin' book

☐ Making a pit stop (ahem, reapplying deodorant—don't be nosy)

☐ Other:

....

....

DOO DOO-DLE

Draw a cute poo!

CREATE AND NAME YOUR DREAM BATHROOM FRESHENER SCENT

.... +
(Part of Speech)

.... +
(Part of Speech)

.... =
(Part of Speech)

....

MOVEMENT METER

How was your poop?

RATE YOUR POOP ON THE SCALE BELOW WITH A HAND-DRAWN POOP EMOJI:

 Dreadfully Dumpy

 Positively Poo-tastic

TOILET PAPER SUPER BOWL

Choose your battle!

CIRCLE ONE:

* SOFTEST FEEL *   * CATCHIEST JINGLE *   * HARDEST WORKING *

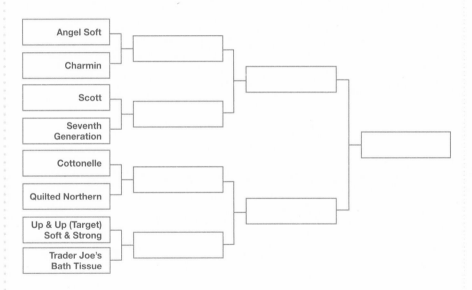

Angel Soft

Charmin

Scott

Seventh Generation

Cottonelle

Quilted Northern

Up & Up (Target) Soft & Strong

Trader Joe's Bath Tissue

...., you're on a roll!

Winning Team

QUALITY ASS-URANCE

How did we doo-doo?

RATE YOUR EXPERIENCE ON A SCALE OF
1 TO 5, 5 MEANING EXTREMELY SATISFIED.

Cleanliness ☆ ☆ ☆ ☆ ☆

Aesthetics ☆ ☆ ☆ ☆ ☆

Toilet Paper ☆ ☆ ☆ ☆ ☆

Spray/SoapScent ☆ ☆ ☆ ☆ ☆

Privacy ☆ ☆ ☆ ☆ ☆

Ventilation ☆ ☆ ☆ ☆ ☆

Plunger Power ☆ ☆ ☆ ☆ ☆

THANKS FOR DROPPING BY

THANKS FOR DROPPING BY

YOUR NAME:

....

IF YOU'RE NOT HERE TO SEE A MAN ABOUT A HORSE, WHAT BROUGHT YOU TO THE LOO?

☐ Just a wiz, lay off!
☐ Freshening up my make-up
☐ Escaping the crowd
☐ Letting out a secret fart or two
☐ Taking a self-guided tour
☐ Signing this stinkin' book
☐ Making a pit stop (ahem, reapplying deodorant—don't be nosy)
☐ Other:

....

DOO DOO-DLE

Draw a cute poo!

CREATE AND NAME YOUR DREAM BATHROOM FRESHENER SCENT

.... +
(Part of Speech)

.... +
(Part of Speech)

.... =
(Part of Speech)

MOVEMENT METER

How was your poop?

RATE YOUR POOP ON THE SCALE BELOW WITH A HAND-DRAWN POOP EMOJI:

 Dreadfully Dumpy

 Positively Poo-tastic

TOILET PAPER SUPER BOWL

Choose your battle!

CIRCLE ONE:
* SOFTEST FEEL *   * CATCHIEST JINGLE *   * HARDEST WORKING *

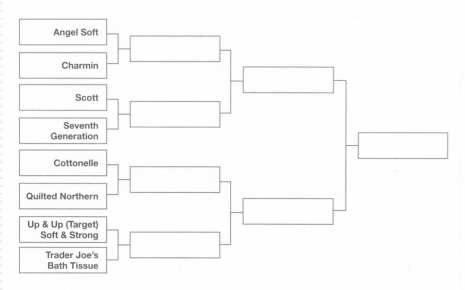

Angel Soft

Charmin

Scott

Seventh Generation

Cottonelle

Quilted Northern

Up & Up (Target) Soft & Strong

Trader Joe's Bath Tissue

...., you're on a roll!

Winning Team

QUALITY ASS-URANCE

How did we doo-doo?

RATE YOUR EXPERIENCE ON A SCALE OF 1 TO 5, 5 MEANING EXTREMELY SATISFIED.

Cleanliness ☆ ☆ ☆ ☆ ☆

Aesthetics ☆ ☆ ☆ ☆ ☆

Toilet Paper ☆ ☆ ☆ ☆ ☆

Spray/SoapScent ☆ ☆ ☆ ☆ ☆

Privacy ☆ ☆ ☆ ☆ ☆

Ventilation ☆ ☆ ☆ ☆ ☆

Plunger Power ☆ ☆ ☆ ☆ ☆

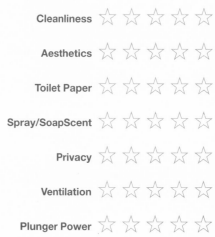

THANKS FOR DROPPING BY

THANKS FOR DROPPING BY

YOUR NAME:

....

IF YOU'RE NOT HERE TO SEE A MAN ABOUT A HORSE, WHAT BROUGHT YOU TO THE LOO?

☐ Just a wiz, lay off!

☐ Freshening up my make-up

☐ Escaping the crowd

☐ Letting out a secret fart or two

☐ Taking a self-guided tour

☐ Signing this stinkin' book

☐ Making a pit stop (ahem, reapplying deodorant—don't be nosy)

☐ Other:

....

....

DOO DOO-DLE

Draw a cute poo!

CREATE AND NAME YOUR DREAM BATHROOM FRESHENER SCENT

.... +
(Part of Speech)

.... +
(Part of Speech)

.... =
(Part of Speech)

....

MOVEMENT METER

How was your poop?

RATE YOUR POOP ON THE SCALE BELOW WITH A HAND-DRAWN POOP EMOJI:

 Dreadfully Dumpy

Positively Poo-tastic

TOILET PAPER SUPER BOWL

Choose your battle!

CIRCLE ONE:
* SOFTEST FEEL *   * CATCHIEST JINGLE *   * HARDEST WORKING *

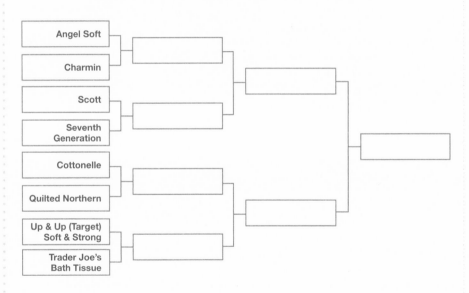

- Angel Soft
- Charmin
- Scott
- Seventh Generation
- Cottonelle
- Quilted Northern
- Up & Up (Target) Soft & Strong
- Trader Joe's Bath Tissue

.... , you're on a roll!

Winning Team

QUALITY ASS-URANCE

How did we doo-doo?

RATE YOUR EXPERIENCE ON A SCALE OF
1 TO 5, 5 MEANING EXTREMELY SATISFIED.

Cleanliness	☆	☆ ☆	☆	☆
Aesthetics	☆	☆ ☆	☆	☆
Toilet Paper	☆	☆ ☆	☆	☆
Spray/SoapScent	☆	☆ ☆	☆	☆
Privacy	☆	☆ ☆	☆	☆
Ventilation	☆	☆ ☆	☆	☆
Plunger Power	☆	☆ ☆	☆	☆

THANKS FOR DROPPING BY

THANKS FOR DROPPING BY

YOUR NAME:

....

IF YOU'RE NOT HERE TO SEE A MAN ABOUT
A HORSE, WHAT BROUGHT YOU TO THE LOO?

☐ Just a wiz, lay off!
☐ Freshening up my make-up
☐ Escaping the crowd
☐ Letting out a secret fart or two
☐ Taking a self-guided tour
☐ Signing this stinkin' book
☐ Making a pit stop (ahem, reapplying
   deodorant—don't be nosy)
☐ Other:

....

....

DOO DOO-DLE

Draw a cute poo!

CREATE AND NAME YOUR DREAM
BATHROOM FRESHENER SCENT

.... +
(Part of Speech)

.... +
(Part of Speech)

.... =
(Part of Speech)

MOVEMENT METER

How was your poop?

RATE YOUR POOP ON THE SCALE BELOW
WITH A HAND-DRAWN POOP EMOJI:

 Dreadfully Dumpy

 Positively Poo-tastic

TOILET PAPER SUPER BOWL

Choose your battle!

CIRCLE ONE:
* SOFTEST FEEL *   * CATCHIEST JINGLE *   * HARDEST WORKING *

Angel Soft

Charmin

Scott

Seventh Generation

Cottonelle

Quilted Northern

Up & Up (Target) Soft & Strong

Trader Joe's Bath Tissue

...., you're on a roll!

Winning Team

QUALITY ASS-URANCE

How did we doo-doo?

**RATE YOUR EXPERIENCE ON A SCALE OF
1 TO 5, 5 MEANING EXTREMELY SATISFIED.**

Cleanliness ☆ ☆ ☆ ☆ ☆

Aesthetics ☆ ☆ ☆ ☆ ☆

Toilet Paper ☆ ☆ ☆ ☆ ☆

Spray/SoapScent ☆ ☆ ☆ ☆ ☆

Privacy ☆ ☆ ☆ ☆ ☆

Ventilation ☆ ☆ ☆ ☆ ☆

Plunger Power ☆ ☆ ☆ ☆ ☆

THANKS FOR DROPPING BY

THANKS FOR DROPPING BY

YOUR NAME:

....

IF YOU'RE NOT HERE TO SEE A MAN ABOUT A HORSE, WHAT BROUGHT YOU TO THE LOO?

☐ Just a wiz, lay off!

☐ Freshening up my make-up

☐ Escaping the crowd

☐ Letting out a secret fart or two

☐ Taking a self-guided tour

☐ Signing this stinkin' book

☐ Making a pit stop (ahem, reapplying deodorant—don't be nosy)

☐ Other:

....

....

DOO DOO-DLE

Draw a cute poo!

CREATE AND NAME YOUR DREAM BATHROOM FRESHENER SCENT

.... +

(Part of Speech)

.... +

(Part of Speech)

.... =

(Part of Speech)

....

MOVEMENT METER

How was your poop?

RATE YOUR POOP ON THE SCALE BELOW WITH A HAND-DRAWN POOP EMOJI:

 Dreadfully Dumpy

 Positively Poo-tastic

TOILET PAPER SUPER BOWL

Choose your battle!

CIRCLE ONE:
* SOFTEST FEEL *   * CATCHIEST JINGLE *   * HARDEST WORKING *

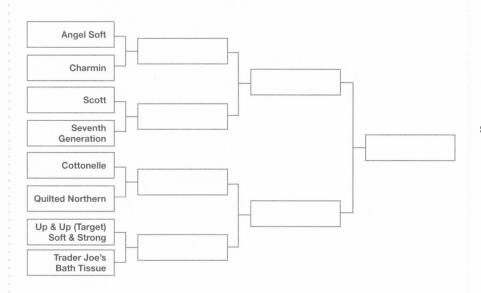

Angel Soft

Charmin

Scott

Seventh Generation

Cottonelle

Quilted Northern

Up & Up (Target) Soft & Strong

Trader Joe's Bath Tissue

.... , you're on a roll!

Winning Team

QUALITY ASS-URANCE

How did we doo-doo?

RATE YOUR EXPERIENCE ON A SCALE OF 1 TO 5, 5 MEANING EXTREMELY SATISFIED.

Cleanliness ☆ ☆ ☆ ☆ ☆

Aesthetics ☆ ☆ ☆ ☆ ☆

Toilet Paper ☆ ☆ ☆ ☆ ☆

Spray/SoapScent ☆ ☆ ☆ ☆ ☆

Privacy ☆ ☆ ☆ ☆ ☆

Ventilation ☆ ☆ ☆ ☆ ☆

Plunger Power ☆ ☆ ☆ ☆ ☆

THANKS FOR DROPPING BY

THANKS FOR DROPPING BY

YOUR NAME:

....

IF YOU'RE NOT HERE TO SEE A MAN ABOUT A HORSE, WHAT BROUGHT YOU TO THE LOO?

☐ Just a wiz, lay off!
☐ Freshening up my make-up
☐ Escaping the crowd
☐ Letting out a secret fart or two
☐ Taking a self-guided tour
☐ Signing this stinkin' book
☐ Making a pit stop (ahem, reapplying deodorant—don't be nosy)
☐ Other:

....

....

DOO DOO-DLE

Draw a cute poo!

CREATE AND NAME YOUR DREAM BATHROOM FRESHENER SCENT

.... +
(Part of Speech)

.... +
(Part of Speech)

.... =
(Part of Speech)

MOVEMENT METER

How was your poop?

RATE YOUR POOP ON THE SCALE BELOW WITH A HAND-DRAWN POOP EMOJI:

 Dreadfully Dumpy

 **Positively Poo-tastic**

TOILET PAPER SUPER BOWL

Choose your battle!

CIRCLE ONE:
* SOFTEST FEEL *   * CATCHIEST JINGLE *   * HARDEST WORKING *

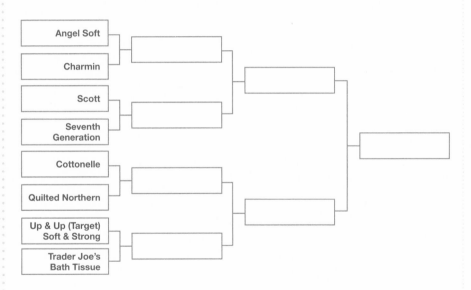

...., you're on a roll!

Winning Team

QUALITY ASS-URANCE

How did we doo-doo?

RATE YOUR EXPERIENCE ON A SCALE OF
1 TO 5, 5 MEANING EXTREMELY SATISFIED.

Cleanliness ☆ ☆ ☆ ☆ ☆

Aesthetics ☆ ☆ ☆ ☆ ☆

Toilet Paper ☆ ☆ ☆ ☆ ☆

Spray/SoapScent ☆ ☆ ☆ ☆ ☆

Privacy ☆ ☆ ☆ ☆ ☆

Ventilation ☆ ☆ ☆ ☆ ☆

Plunger Power ☆ ☆ ☆ ☆ ☆

THANKS FOR DROPPING BY

THANKS FOR DROPPING BY

YOUR NAME:

....

IF YOU'RE NOT HERE TO SEE A MAN ABOUT
A HORSE, WHAT BROUGHT YOU TO THE LOO?

☐ Just a wiz, lay off!
☐ Freshening up my make-up
☐ Escaping the crowd
☐ Letting out a secret fart or two
☐ Taking a self-guided tour
☐ Signing this stinkin' book
☐ Making a pit stop (ahem, reapplying
　 deodorant—don't be nosy)
☐ Other:

....

....

DOO DOO-DLE

Draw a cute poo!

**CREATE AND NAME YOUR DREAM
BATHROOM FRESHENER SCENT**

.... +
(Part of Speech)

.... +
(Part of Speech)

.... =
(Part of Speech)

....

MOVEMENT METER

How was your poop?

**RATE YOUR POOP ON THE SCALE BELOW
WITH A HAND-DRAWN POOP EMOJI:**

 Dreadfully Dumpy

 Positively Poo-tastic

TOILET PAPER SUPER BOWL

Choose your battle!

CIRCLE ONE:
* SOFTEST FEEL *   * CATCHIEST JINGLE *   * HARDEST WORKING *

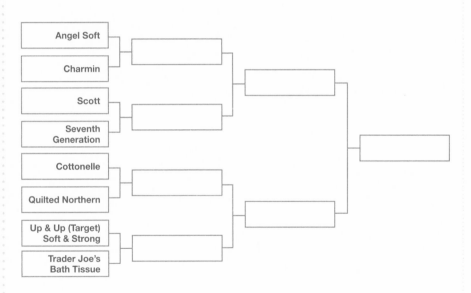

Angel Soft

Charmin

Scott

Seventh Generation

Cottonelle

Quilted Northern

Up & Up (Target) Soft & Strong

Trader Joe's Bath Tissue

...., you're on a roll!

Winning Team

QUALITY ASS-URANCE

How did we doo-doo?

RATE YOUR EXPERIENCE ON A SCALE OF 1 TO 5, 5 MEANING EXTREMELY SATISFIED.

Cleanliness ☆ ☆ ☆ ☆ ☆

Aesthetics ☆ ☆ ☆ ☆ ☆

Toilet Paper ☆ ☆ ☆ ☆ ☆

Spray/SoapScent ☆ ☆ ☆ ☆ ☆

Privacy ☆ ☆ ☆ ☆ ☆

Ventilation ☆ ☆ ☆ ☆ ☆

Plunger Power ☆ ☆ ☆ ☆ ☆

THANKS FOR DROPPING BY

THANKS FOR DROPPING BY

YOUR NAME:

....

IF YOU'RE NOT HERE TO SEE A MAN ABOUT A HORSE, WHAT BROUGHT YOU TO THE LOO?

☐ Just a wiz, lay off!
☐ Freshening up my make-up
☐ Escaping the crowd
☐ Letting out a secret fart or two
☐ Taking a self-guided tour
☐ Signing this stinkin' book
☐ Making a pit stop (ahem, reapplying deodorant—don't be nosy)
☐ Other:

....

....

DOO DOO-DLE

Draw a cute poo!

CREATE AND NAME YOUR DREAM BATHROOM FRESHENER SCENT

.... +
(Part of Speech)

.... +
(Part of Speech)

.... =
(Part of Speech)

MOVEMENT METER

How was your poop?

RATE YOUR POOP ON THE SCALE BELOW WITH A HAND-DRAWN POOP EMOJI:

 Dreadfully Dumpy

 Positively Poo-tastic

TOILET PAPER SUPER BOWL

Choose your battle!

CIRCLE ONE:
* SOFTEST FEEL *   * CATCHIEST JINGLE *   * HARDEST WORKING *

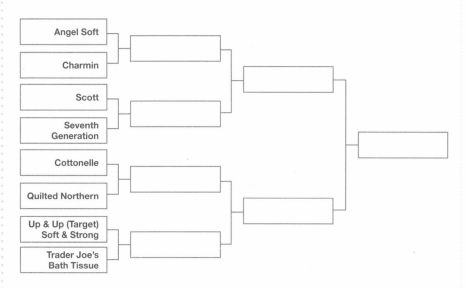

Angel Soft

Charmin

Scott

Seventh Generation

Cottonelle

Quilted Northern

Up & Up (Target) Soft & Strong

Trader Joe's Bath Tissue

...., you're on a roll!

Winning Team

QUALITY ASS-URANCE

How did we doo-doo?

RATE YOUR EXPERIENCE ON A SCALE OF
1 TO 5, 5 MEANING EXTREMELY SATISFIED.

Cleanliness ☆ ☆ ☆ ☆ ☆

Aesthetics ☆ ☆ ☆ ☆ ☆

Toilet Paper ☆ ☆ ☆ ☆ ☆

Spray/SoapScent ☆ ☆ ☆ ☆ ☆

Privacy ☆ ☆ ☆ ☆ ☆

Ventilation ☆ ☆ ☆ ☆ ☆

Plunger Power ☆ ☆ ☆ ☆ ☆

THANKS FOR DROPPING BY

THANKS FOR DROPPING BY

YOUR NAME:

....

IF YOU'RE NOT HERE TO SEE A MAN ABOUT A HORSE, WHAT BROUGHT YOU TO THE LOO?

☐ Just a wiz, lay off!

☐ Freshening up my make-up

☐ Escaping the crowd

☐ Letting out a secret fart or two

☐ Taking a self-guided tour

☐ Signing this stinkin' book

☐ Making a pit stop (ahem, reapplying deodorant—don't be nosy)

☐ Other:

....

....

DOO DOO-DLE

Draw a cute poo!

CREATE AND NAME YOUR DREAM BATHROOM FRESHENER SCENT

.... +
(Part of Speech)

.... +
(Part of Speech)

.... =
(Part of Speech)

....

MOVEMENT METER

How was your poop?

RATE YOUR POOP ON THE SCALE BELOW WITH A HAND-DRAWN POOP EMOJI:

 Dreadfully Dumpy

Positively Poo-tastic

TOILET PAPER SUPER BOWL

Choose your battle!

CIRCLE ONE:
* SOFTEST FEEL *   * CATCHIEST JINGLE *   * HARDEST WORKING *

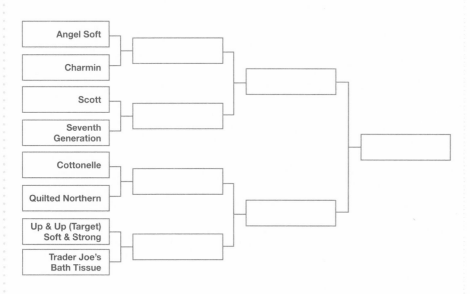

Angel Soft

Charmin

Scott

Seventh Generation

Cottonelle

Quilted Northern

Up & Up (Target) Soft & Strong

Trader Joe's Bath Tissue

.... , you're on a roll!

Winning Team

QUALITY ASS-URANCE

How did we doo-doo?

RATE YOUR EXPERIENCE ON A SCALE OF 1 TO 5, 5 MEANING EXTREMELY SATISFIED.

Cleanliness ☆ ☆ ☆ ☆ ☆

Aesthetics ☆ ☆ ☆ ☆ ☆

Toilet Paper ☆ ☆ ☆ ☆ ☆

Spray/SoapScent ☆ ☆ ☆ ☆ ☆

Privacy ☆ ☆ ☆ ☆ ☆

Ventilation ☆ ☆ ☆ ☆ ☆

Plunger Power ☆ ☆ ☆ ☆ ☆

THANKS FOR DROPPING BY

THANKS FOR DROPPING BY

YOUR NAME:

....

IF YOU'RE NOT HERE TO SEE A MAN ABOUT A HORSE, WHAT BROUGHT YOU TO THE LOO?

☐ Just a wiz, lay off!

☐ Freshening up my make-up

☐ Escaping the crowd

☐ Letting out a secret fart or two

☐ Taking a self-guided tour

☐ Signing this stinkin' book

☐ Making a pit stop (ahem, reapplying deodorant—don't be nosy)

☐ Other:

....

....

DOO DOO-DLE

Draw a cute poo!

CREATE AND NAME YOUR DREAM BATHROOM FRESHENER SCENT

.... +
(Part of Speech)

.... +
(Part of Speech)

.... =
(Part of Speech)

MOVEMENT METER

How was your poop?

RATE YOUR POOP ON THE SCALE BELOW WITH A HAND-DRAWN POOP EMOJI:

 Dreadfully Dumpy

Positively Poo-tastic

TOILET PAPER SUPER BOWL

Choose your battle!

CIRCLE ONE:
* SOFTEST FEEL *   * CATCHIEST JINGLE *   * HARDEST WORKING *

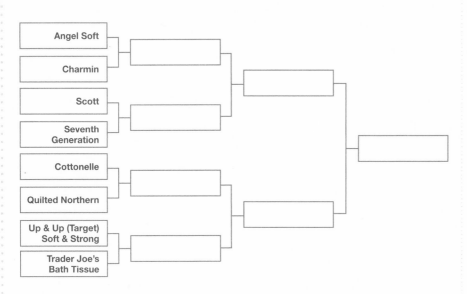

- Angel Soft
- Charmin
- Scott
- Seventh Generation
- Cottonelle
- Quilted Northern
- Up & Up (Target) Soft & Strong
- Trader Joe's Bath Tissue

...., you're on a roll!

Winning Team

QUALITY ASS-URANCE

How did we doo-doo?

RATE YOUR EXPERIENCE ON A SCALE OF
1 TO 5, 5 MEANING EXTREMELY SATISFIED.

Cleanliness ☆ ☆ ☆ ☆ ☆

Aesthetics ☆ ☆ ☆ ☆ ☆

Toilet Paper ☆ ☆ ☆ ☆ ☆

Spray/SoapScent ☆ ☆ ☆ ☆ ☆

Privacy ☆ ☆ ☆ ☆ ☆

Ventilation ☆ ☆ ☆ ☆ ☆

Plunger Power ☆ ☆ ☆ ☆ ☆

THANKS FOR DROPPING BY

THANKS FOR DROPPING BY

YOUR NAME:

....

IF YOU'RE NOT HERE TO SEE A MAN ABOUT A HORSE, WHAT BROUGHT YOU TO THE LOO?

☐ Just a wiz, lay off!

☐ Freshening up my make-up

☐ Escaping the crowd

☐ Letting out a secret fart or two

☐ Taking a self-guided tour

☐ Signing this stinkin' book

☐ Making a pit stop (ahem, reapplying deodorant—don't be nosy)

☐ Other:

....

....

DOO DOO-DLE

Draw a cute poo!

CREATE AND NAME YOUR DREAM BATHROOM FRESHENER SCENT

.... +

(Part of Speech)

.... +

(Part of Speech)

.... =

(Part of Speech)

MOVEMENT METER

How was your poop?

RATE YOUR POOP ON THE SCALE BELOW WITH A HAND-DRAWN POOP EMOJI:

 Dreadfully Dumpy

 Positively Poo-tastic

TOILET PAPER SUPER BOWL

Choose your battle!

CIRCLE ONE:
* SOFTEST FEEL *   * CATCHIEST JINGLE *   * HARDEST WORKING *

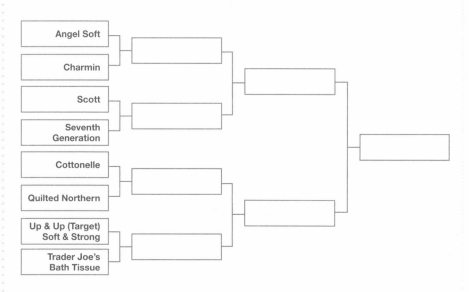

Angel Soft	
Charmin	
Scott	
Seventh Generation	
Cottonelle	
Quilted Northern	
Up & Up (Target) Soft & Strong	
Trader Joe's Bath Tissue	

...., you're on a roll!

Winning Team

QUALITY ASS-URANCE

How did we doo-doo?

RATE YOUR EXPERIENCE ON A SCALE OF
1 TO 5, 5 MEANING EXTREMELY SATISFIED.

Cleanliness ☆ ☆ ☆ ☆ ☆

Aesthetics ☆ ☆ ☆ ☆ ☆

Toilet Paper ☆ ☆ ☆ ☆ ☆

Spray/SoapScent ☆ ☆ ☆ ☆ ☆

Privacy ☆ ☆ ☆ ☆ ☆

Ventilation ☆ ☆ ☆ ☆ ☆

Plunger Power ☆ ☆ ☆ ☆ ☆

THANKS FOR DROPPING BY

THANKS FOR DROPPING BY

YOUR NAME:

....

IF YOU'RE NOT HERE TO SEE A MAN ABOUT A HORSE, WHAT BROUGHT YOU TO THE LOO?

☐ Just a wiz, lay off!

☐ Freshening up my make-up

☐ Escaping the crowd

☐ Letting out a secret fart or two

☐ Taking a self-guided tour

☐ Signing this stinkin' book

☐ Making a pit stop (ahem, reapplying deodorant—don't be nosy)

☐ Other:

....

....

DOO DOO-DLE

Draw a cute poo!

CREATE AND NAME YOUR DREAM BATHROOM FRESHENER SCENT

.... +

(Part of Speech)

.... +

(Part of Speech)

.... =

(Part of Speech)

MOVEMENT METER

How was your poop?

RATE YOUR POOP ON THE SCALE BELOW WITH A HAND-DRAWN POOP EMOJI:

 Dreadfully Dumpy

 Positively Poo-tastic

TOILET PAPER SUPER BOWL

Choose your battle!

CIRCLE ONE:
* SOFTEST FEEL *   * CATCHIEST JINGLE *   * HARDEST WORKING *

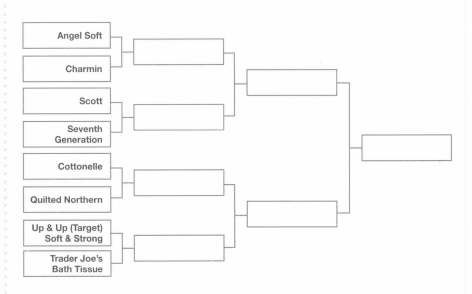

Angel Soft

Charmin

Scott

Seventh Generation

Cottonelle

Quilted Northern

Up & Up (Target) Soft & Strong

Trader Joe's Bath Tissue

.... , you're on a roll!

Winning Team

QUALITY ASS-URANCE

How did we doo-doo?

RATE YOUR EXPERIENCE ON A SCALE OF 1 TO 5, 5 MEANING EXTREMELY SATISFIED.

Cleanliness ☆ ☆ ☆ ☆ ☆

Aesthetics ☆ ☆ ☆ ☆ ☆

Toilet Paper ☆ ☆ ☆ ☆ ☆

Spray/SoapScent ☆ ☆ ☆ ☆ ☆

Privacy ☆ ☆ ☆ ☆ ☆

Ventilation ☆ ☆ ☆ ☆ ☆

Plunger Power ☆ ☆ ☆ ☆ ☆

THANKS FOR DROPPING BY

THANKS FOR DROPPING BY

YOUR NAME:

....

IF YOU'RE NOT HERE TO SEE A MAN ABOUT A HORSE, WHAT BROUGHT YOU TO THE LOO?

☐ Just a wiz, lay off!
☐ Freshening up my make-up
☐ Escaping the crowd
☐ Letting out a secret fart or two
☐ Taking a self-guided tour
☐ Signing this stinkin' book
☐ Making a pit stop (ahem, reapplying deodorant—don't be nosy)
☐ Other:

....

....

DOO DOO-DLE

Draw a cute poo!

CREATE AND NAME YOUR DREAM BATHROOM FRESHENER SCENT

.... +

(Part of Speech)

.... +

(Part of Speech)

.... =

(Part of Speech)

....

MOVEMENT METER

How was your poop?

RATE YOUR POOP ON THE SCALE BELOW WITH A HAND-DRAWN POOP EMOJI:

 Dreadfully Dumpy

Positively Poo-tastic

TOILET PAPER SUPER BOWL

Choose your battle!

CIRCLE ONE:
* SOFTEST FEEL *   * CATCHIEST JINGLE *   * HARDEST WORKING *

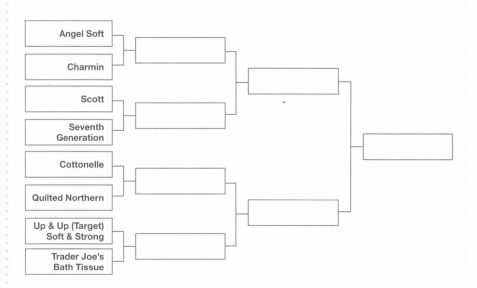

Angel Soft

Charmin

Scott

Seventh Generation

Cottonelle

Quilted Northern

Up & Up (Target) Soft & Strong

Trader Joe's Bath Tissue

.... , you're on a roll!

Winning Team

QUALITY ASS-URANCE

How did we doo-doo?

RATE YOUR EXPERIENCE ON A SCALE OF
1 TO 5, 5 MEANING EXTREMELY SATISFIED.

Cleanliness ☆ ☆ ☆ ☆ ☆

Aesthetics ☆ ☆ ☆ ☆ ☆

Toilet Paper ☆ ☆ ☆ ☆ ☆

Spray/SoapScent ☆ ☆ ☆ ☆ ☆

Privacy ☆ ☆ ☆ ☆ ☆

Ventilation ☆ ☆ ☆ ☆ ☆

Plunger Power ☆ ☆ ☆ ☆ ☆

THANKS FOR DROPPING BY

THANKS FOR DROPPING BY

YOUR NAME:

....

IF YOU'RE NOT HERE TO SEE A MAN ABOUT A HORSE, WHAT BROUGHT YOU TO THE LOO?

☐ Just a wiz, lay off!
☐ Freshening up my make-up
☐ Escaping the crowd
☐ Letting out a secret fart or two
☐ Taking a self-guided tour
☐ Signing this stinkin' book
☐ Making a pit stop (ahem, reapplying deodorant—don't be nosy)
☐ Other:

....

....

DOO DOO-DLE

Draw a cute poo!

CREATE AND NAME YOUR DREAM BATHROOM FRESHENER SCENT

.... +
(Part of Speech)

.... +
(Part of Speech)

.... =
(Part of Speech)

MOVEMENT METER

How was your poop?

RATE YOUR POOP ON THE SCALE BELOW WITH A HAND-DRAWN POOP EMOJI:

 Dreadfully Dumpy

 Positively Poo-tastic

TOILET PAPER SUPER BOWL

Choose your battle!

CIRCLE ONE:
* SOFTEST FEEL *   * CATCHIEST JINGLE *   * HARDEST WORKING *

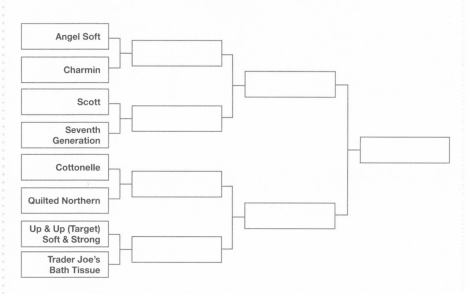

- Angel Soft
- Charmin
- Scott
- Seventh Generation
- Cottonelle
- Quilted Northern
- Up & Up (Target) Soft & Strong
- Trader Joe's Bath Tissue

.... , you're on a roll!

Winning Team

QUALITY ASS-URANCE

How did we doo-doo?

RATE YOUR EXPERIENCE ON A SCALE OF · 1 TO 5, 5 MEANING EXTREMELY SATISFIED.

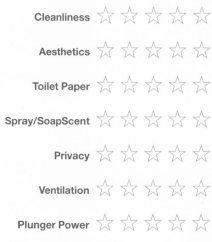

Cleanliness ☆ ☆ ☆ ☆ ☆

Aesthetics ☆ ☆ ☆ ☆ ☆

Toilet Paper ☆ ☆ ☆ ☆ ☆

Spray/SoapScent ☆ ☆ ☆ ☆ ☆

Privacy ☆ ☆ ☆ ☆ ☆

Ventilation ☆ ☆ ☆ ☆ ☆

Plunger Power ☆ ☆ ☆ ☆ ☆

THANKS FOR DROPPING BY

THANKS FOR DROPPING BY

YOUR NAME:

....

IF YOU'RE NOT HERE TO SEE A MAN ABOUT A HORSE, WHAT BROUGHT YOU TO THE LOO?

☐ Just a wiz, lay off!

☐ Freshening up my make-up

☐ Escaping the crowd

☐ Letting out a secret fart or two

☐ Taking a self-guided tour

☐ Signing this stinkin' book

☐ Making a pit stop (ahem, reapplying deodorant—don't be nosy)

☐ Other:

....

....

DOO DOO-DLE

Draw a cute poo!

CREATE AND NAME YOUR DREAM BATHROOM FRESHENER SCENT

.... +
(Part of Speech)

.... +
(Part of Speech)

.... =
(Part of Speech)

MOVEMENT METER

How was your poop?

RATE YOUR POOP ON THE SCALE BELOW WITH A HAND-DRAWN POOP EMOJI:

 Dreadfully Dumpy

Positively Poo-tastic

TOILET PAPER SUPER BOWL

Choose your battle!

CIRCLE ONE:
* SOFTEST FEEL *   * CATCHIEST JINGLE *   * HARDEST WORKING *

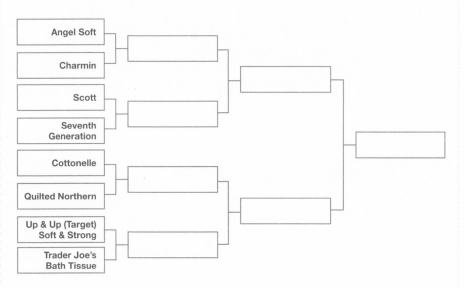

- Angel Soft
- Charmin
- Scott
- Seventh Generation
- Cottonelle
- Quilted Northern
- Up & Up (Target) Soft & Strong
- Trader Joe's Bath Tissue

.... , you're on a roll!

Winning Team

QUALITY ASS-URANCE

How did we doo-doo?

RATE YOUR EXPERIENCE ON A SCALE OF
1 TO 5, 5 MEANING EXTREMELY SATISFIED.

Cleanliness ☆ ☆ ☆ ☆ ☆

Aesthetics ☆ ☆ ☆ ☆ ☆

Toilet Paper ☆ ☆ ☆ ☆ ☆

Spray/SoapScent ☆ ☆ ☆ ☆ ☆

Privacy ☆ ☆ ☆ ☆ ☆

Ventilation ☆ ☆ ☆ ☆ ☆

Plunger Power ☆ ☆ ☆ ☆ ☆

THANKS FOR DROPPING BY

THANKS FOR DROPPING BY

YOUR NAME:

....

IF YOU'RE NOT HERE TO SEE A MAN ABOUT A HORSE, WHAT BROUGHT YOU TO THE LOO?

☐ Just a wiz, lay off!

☐ Freshening up my make-up

☐ Escaping the crowd

☐ Letting out a secret fart or two

☐ Taking a self-guided tour

☐ Signing this stinkin' book

☐ Making a pit stop (ahem, reapplying deodorant—don't be nosy)

☐ Other:

....

DOO DOO-DLE

Draw a cute poo!

CREATE AND NAME YOUR DREAM BATHROOM FRESHENER SCENT

.... +

(Part of Speech)

.... +

(Part of Speech)

.... =

(Part of Speech)

MOVEMENT METER

How was your poop?

RATE YOUR POOP ON THE SCALE BELOW WITH A HAND-DRAWN POOP EMOJI:

 Dreadfully Dumpy

 Positively Poo-tastic

TOILET PAPER SUPER BOWL

Choose your battle!

CIRCLE ONE:
* SOFTEST FEEL * * CATCHIEST JINGLE * * HARDEST WORKING *

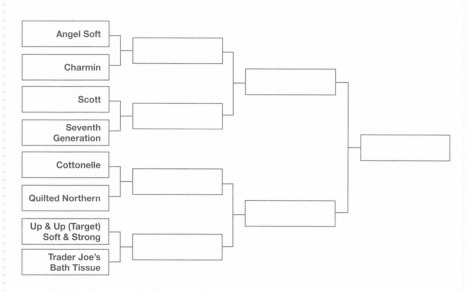

Angel Soft

Charmin

Scott

Seventh Generation

Cottonelle

Quilted Northern

Up & Up (Target) Soft & Strong

Trader Joe's Bath Tissue

.... , you're on a roll!

Winning Team

QUALITY ASS·URANCE

How did we doo-doo?

RATE YOUR EXPERIENCE ON A SCALE OF 1 TO 5, 5 MEANING EXTREMELY SATISFIED.

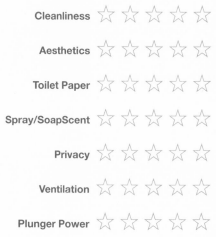

Cleanliness ☆ ☆ ☆ ☆ ☆

Aesthetics ☆ ☆ ☆ ☆ ☆

Toilet Paper ☆ ☆ ☆ ☆ ☆

Spray/SoapScent ☆ ☆ ☆ ☆ ☆

Privacy ☆ ☆ ☆ ☆ ☆

Ventilation ☆ ☆ ☆ ☆ ☆

Plunger Power ☆ ☆ ☆ ☆ ☆

THANKS FOR DROPPING BY

THANKS FOR DROPPING BY

YOUR NAME:

....

IF YOU'RE NOT HERE TO SEE A MAN ABOUT A HORSE, WHAT BROUGHT YOU TO THE LOO?

☐ Just a wiz, lay off!
☐ Freshening up my make-up
☐ Escaping the crowd
☐ Letting out a secret fart or two
☐ Taking a self-guided tour
☐ Signing this stinkin' book
☐ Making a pit stop (ahem, reapplying deodorant—don't be nosy)
☐ Other:

....

....

DOO DOO-DLE

Draw a cute poo!

CREATE AND NAME YOUR DREAM BATHROOM FRESHENER SCENT

.... +
(Part of Speech)

.... +
(Part of Speech)

.... =
(Part of Speech)

MOVEMENT METER

How was your poop?

RATE YOUR POOP ON THE SCALE BELOW WITH A HAND-DRAWN POOP EMOJI:

 Dreadfully Dumpy

Positively Poo-tastic

TOILET PAPER SUPER BOWL

Choose your battle!

CIRCLE ONE:
* SOFTEST FEEL *   * CATCHIEST JINGLE *   * HARDEST WORKING *

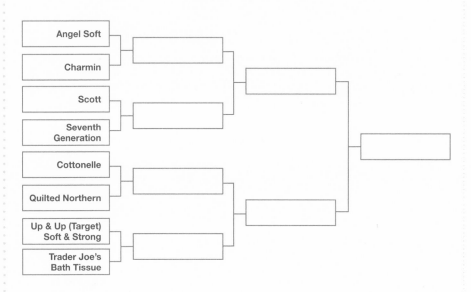

Angel Soft

Charmin

Scott

Seventh
Generation

Cottonelle

Quilted Northern

Up & Up (Target)
Soft & Strong

Trader Joe's
Bath Tissue

.... , you're on a roll!

Winning Team

QUALITY ASS-URANCE

How did we doo-doo?

RATE YOUR EXPERIENCE ON A SCALE OF
1 TO 5, 5 MEANING EXTREMELY SATISFIED.

Cleanliness ☆ ☆ ☆ ☆ ☆

Aesthetics ☆ ☆ ☆ ☆ ☆

Toilet Paper ☆ ☆ ☆ ☆ ☆

Spray/SoapScent ☆ ☆ ☆ ☆ ☆

Privacy ☆ ☆ ☆ ☆ ☆

Ventilation ☆ ☆ ☆ ☆ ☆

Plunger Power ☆ ☆ ☆ ☆ ☆

THANKS FOR
DROPPING BY

THANKS FOR DROPPING BY

YOUR NAME:

....

IF YOU'RE NOT HERE TO SEE A MAN ABOUT A HORSE, WHAT BROUGHT YOU TO THE LOO?

☐ Just a wiz, lay off!

☐ Freshening up my make-up

☐ Escaping the crowd

☐ Letting out a secret fart or two

☐ Taking a self-guided tour

☐ Signing this stinkin' book

☐ Making a pit stop (ahem, reapplying deodorant—don't be nosy)

☐ Other:

....

DOO DOO-DLE

Draw a cute poo!

CREATE AND NAME YOUR DREAM BATHROOM FRESHENER SCENT

.... +

(Part of Speech)

.... +

(Part of Speech)

.... =

(Part of Speech)

MOVEMENT METER

How was your poop?

RATE YOUR POOP ON THE SCALE BELOW WITH A HAND-DRAWN POOP EMOJI:

 Dreadfully Dumpy

 Positively Poo-tastic

TOILET PAPER SUPER BOWL

Choose your battle!

CIRCLE ONE:
* SOFTEST FEEL *   * CATCHIEST JINGLE *   * HARDEST WORKING *

Angel Soft

Charmin

Scott

Seventh Generation

Cottonelle

Quilted Northern

Up & Up (Target) Soft & Strong

Trader Joe's Bath Tissue

...., you're on a roll!

Winning Team

QUALITY ASS·URANCE

How did we doo-doo?

RATE YOUR EXPERIENCE ON A SCALE OF
1 TO 5, 5 MEANING EXTREMELY SATISFIED.

Cleanliness ☆ ☆ ☆ ☆ ☆

Aesthetics ☆ ☆ ☆ ☆ ☆

Toilet Paper ☆ ☆ ☆ ☆ ☆

Spray/SoapScent ☆ ☆ ☆ ☆ ☆

Privacy ☆ ☆ ☆ ☆ ☆

Ventilation ☆ ☆ ☆ ☆ ☆

Plunger Power ☆ ☆ ☆ ☆ ☆

THANKS FOR DROPPING BY

THANKS FOR DROPPING BY

YOUR NAME:

....

IF YOU'RE NOT HERE TO SEE A MAN ABOUT A HORSE, WHAT BROUGHT YOU TO THE LOO?

☐ Just a wiz, lay off!

☐ Freshening up my make-up

☐ Escaping the crowd

☐ Letting out a secret fart or two

☐ Taking a self-guided tour

☐ Signing this stinkin' book

☐ Making a pit stop (ahem, reapplying deodorant—don't be nosy)

☐ Other:

....

DOO DOO-DLE

Draw a cute poo!

CREATE AND NAME YOUR DREAM BATHROOM FRESHENER SCENT

.... +
(Part of Speech)

.... +
(Part of Speech)

.... =
(Part of Speech)

MOVEMENT METER

How was your poop?

RATE YOUR POOP ON THE SCALE BELOW WITH A HAND-DRAWN POOP EMOJI:

 Dreadfully Dumpy

Positively Poo-tastic

TOILET PAPER SUPER BOWL

Choose your battle!

CIRCLE ONE:
* SOFTEST FEEL *   * CATCHIEST JINGLE *   * HARDEST WORKING *

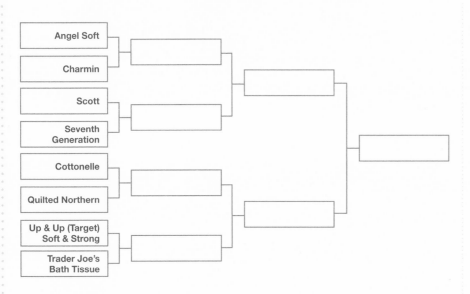

Angel Soft

Charmin

Scott

Seventh Generation

Cottonelle

Quilted Northern

Up & Up (Target) Soft & Strong

Trader Joe's Bath Tissue

.... , you're on a roll!

Winning Team

QUALITY ASS-URANCE

How did we doo-doo?

RATE YOUR EXPERIENCE ON A SCALE OF 1 TO 5, 5 MEANING EXTREMELY SATISFIED.

Cleanliness ☆ ☆ ☆ ☆ ☆

Aesthetics ☆ ☆ ☆ ☆ ☆

Toilet Paper ☆ ☆ ☆ ☆ ☆

Spray/SoapScent ☆ ☆ ☆ ☆ ☆

Privacy ☆ ☆ ☆ ☆ ☆

Ventilation ☆ ☆ ☆ ☆ ☆

Plunger Power ☆ ☆ ☆ ☆ ☆

THANKS FOR DROPPING BY

THANKS FOR DROPPING BY

YOUR NAME:

....

IF YOU'RE NOT HERE TO SEE A MAN ABOUT A HORSE, WHAT BROUGHT YOU TO THE LOO?

☐ Just a wiz, lay off!
☐ Freshening up my make-up
☐ Escaping the crowd
☐ Letting out a secret fart or two
☐ Taking a self-guided tour
☐ Signing this stinkin' book
☐ Making a pit stop (ahem, reapplying deodorant—don't be nosy)
☐ Other:

....

....

DOO DOO-DLE

Draw a cute poo!

CREATE AND NAME YOUR DREAM BATHROOM FRESHENER SCENT

.... +
(Part of Speech)

.... +
(Part of Speech)

.... =
(Part of Speech)

....

MOVEMENT METER

How was your poop?

RATE YOUR POOP ON THE SCALE BELOW WITH A HAND-DRAWN POOP EMOJI:

 Dreadfully Dumpy

 **Positively Poo-tastic**

TOILET PAPER SUPER BOWL

Choose your battle!

CIRCLE ONE:
* SOFTEST FEEL *   * CATCHIEST JINGLE *   * HARDEST WORKING *

Angel Soft

Charmin

Scott

Seventh Generation

Cottonelle

Quilted Northern

Up & Up (Target) Soft & Strong

Trader Joe's Bath Tissue

.... , you're on a roll!

Winning Team

QUALITY ASS-URANCE

How did we doo-doo?

RATE YOUR EXPERIENCE ON A SCALE OF
1 TO 5, 5 MEANING EXTREMELY SATISFIED.

Cleanliness ☆ ☆ ☆ ☆ ☆

Aesthetics ☆ ☆ ☆ ☆ ☆

Toilet Paper ☆ ☆ ☆ ☆ ☆

Spray/SoapScent ☆ ☆ ☆ ☆ ☆

Privacy ☆ ☆ ☆ ☆ ☆

Ventilation ☆ ☆ ☆ ☆ ☆

Plunger Power ☆ ☆ ☆ ☆ ☆

THANKS FOR DROPPING BY

THANKS FOR DROPPING BY

YOUR NAME:

....

IF YOU'RE NOT HERE TO SEE A MAN ABOUT A HORSE, WHAT BROUGHT YOU TO THE LOO?

☐ Just a wiz, lay off!
☐ Freshening up my make-up
☐ Escaping the crowd
☐ Letting out a secret fart or two
☐ Taking a self-guided tour
☐ Signing this stinkin' book
☐ Making a pit stop (ahem, reapplying deodorant—don't be nosy)
☐ Other:

....

....

DOO DOO-DLE

Draw a cute poo!

CREATE AND NAME YOUR DREAM BATHROOM FRESHENER SCENT

.... +
(Part of Speech)

.... +
(Part of Speech)

.... =
(Part of Speech)

....

MOVEMENT METER

How was your poop?

RATE YOUR POOP ON THE SCALE BELOW WITH A HAND-DRAWN POOP EMOJI:

 Dreadfully Dumpy

 Positively Poo-tastic

TOILET PAPER SUPER BOWL

Choose your battle!

CIRCLE ONE:
* SOFTEST FEEL * *** CATCHIEST JINGLE *** *** HARDEST WORKING ***

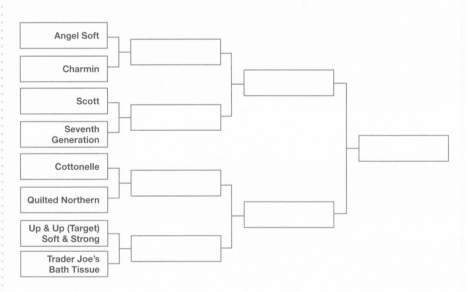

Angel Soft

Charmin

Scott

Seventh Generation

Cottonelle

Quilted Northern

Up & Up (Target) Soft & Strong

Trader Joe's Bath Tissue

.... , you're on a roll!

Winning Team

QUALITY ASS-URANCE

How did we doo-doo?

RATE YOUR EXPERIENCE ON A SCALE OF 1 TO 5, 5 MEANING EXTREMELY SATISFIED.

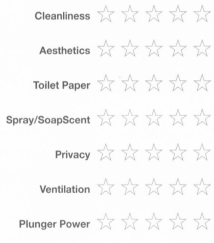

Cleanliness ☆ ☆ ☆ ☆ ☆

Aesthetics ☆ ☆ ☆ ☆ ☆

Toilet Paper ☆ ☆ ☆ ☆ ☆

Spray/SoapScent ☆ ☆ ☆ ☆ ☆

Privacy ☆ ☆ ☆ ☆ ☆

Ventilation ☆ ☆ ☆ ☆ ☆

Plunger Power ☆ ☆ ☆ ☆ ☆

THANKS FOR DROPPING BY

THANKS FOR DROPPING BY

YOUR NAME:

....

IF YOU'RE NOT HERE TO SEE A MAN ABOUT A HORSE, WHAT BROUGHT YOU TO THE LOO?

☐ Just a wiz, lay off!
☐ Freshening up my make-up
☐ Escaping the crowd
☐ Letting out a secret fart or two
☐ Taking a self-guided tour
☐ Signing this stinkin' book
☐ Making a pit stop (ahem, reapplying deodorant—don't be nosy)
☐ Other:

....

....

DOO DOO-DLE

Draw a cute poo!

CREATE AND NAME YOUR DREAM BATHROOM FRESHENER SCENT

.... +
(Part of Speech)

.... +
(Part of Speech)

.... =
(Part of Speech)

MOVEMENT METER

How was your poop?

RATE YOUR POOP ON THE SCALE BELOW WITH A HAND-DRAWN POOP EMOJI:

 Dreadfully Dumpy

Positively Poo-tastic

TOILET PAPER SUPER BOWL

Choose your battle!

CIRCLE ONE:
* SOFTEST FEEL *   * CATCHIEST JINGLE *   * HARDEST WORKING *

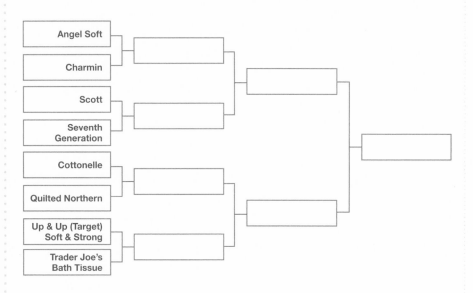

- Angel Soft
- Charmin
- Scott
- Seventh Generation
- Cottonelle
- Quilted Northern
- Up & Up (Target) Soft & Strong
- Trader Joe's Bath Tissue

.... , you're on a roll!

Winning Team

QUALITY ASS-URANCE

How did we doo-doo?

RATE YOUR EXPERIENCE ON A SCALE OF 1 TO 5, 5 MEANING EXTREMELY SATISFIED.

Cleanliness ☆ ☆ ☆ ☆ ☆

Aesthetics ☆ ☆ ☆ ☆ ☆

Toilet Paper ☆ ☆ ☆ ☆ ☆

Spray/SoapScent ☆ ☆ ☆ ☆ ☆

Privacy ☆ ☆ ☆ ☆ ☆

Ventilation ☆ ☆ ☆ ☆ ☆

Plunger Power ☆ ☆ ☆ ☆ ☆

THANKS FOR DROPPING BY

THANKS FOR DROPPING BY

YOUR NAME:

....

IF YOU'RE NOT HERE TO SEE A MAN ABOUT A HORSE, WHAT BROUGHT YOU TO THE LOO?

☐ Just a wiz, lay off!
☐ Freshening up my make-up
☐ Escaping the crowd
☐ Letting out a secret fart or two
☐ Taking a self-guided tour
☐ Signing this stinkin' book
☐ Making a pit stop (ahem, reapplying deodorant—don't be nosy)
☐ Other:

....

....

DOO DOO-DLE

Draw a cute poo!

CREATE AND NAME YOUR DREAM BATHROOM FRESHENER SCENT

.... +
(Part of Speech)

.... +
(Part of Speech)

.... =
(Part of Speech)

....

MOVEMENT METER

How was your poop?

RATE YOUR POOP ON THE SCALE BELOW WITH A HAND-DRAWN POOP EMOJI:

 Dreadfully Dumpy

Positively Poo-tastic

TOILET PAPER SUPER BOWL

Choose your battle!

CIRCLE ONE:
* SOFTEST FEEL *   * CATCHIEST JINGLE *   * HARDEST WORKING *

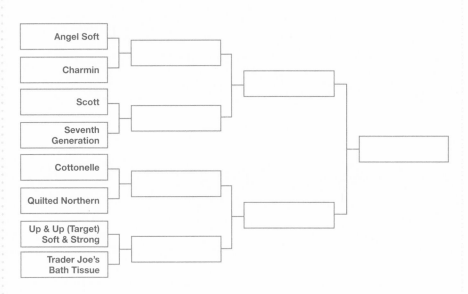

Angel Soft

Charmin

Scott

Seventh Generation

Cottonelle

Quilted Northern

Up & Up (Target) Soft & Strong

Trader Joe's Bath Tissue

.... , you're on a roll!

Winning Team

QUALITY ASS-URANCE

How did we doo-doo?

RATE YOUR EXPERIENCE ON A SCALE OF 1 TO 5, 5 MEANING EXTREMELY SATISFIED.

Cleanliness ☆ ☆ ☆ ☆ ☆

Aesthetics ☆ ☆ ☆ ☆ ☆

Toilet Paper ☆ ☆ ☆ ☆ ☆

Spray/SoapScent ☆ ☆ ☆ ☆ ☆

Privacy ☆ ☆ ☆ ☆ ☆

Ventilation ☆ ☆ ☆ ☆ ☆

Plunger Power ☆ ☆ ☆ ☆ ☆

THANKS FOR DROPPING BY

THANKS FOR DROPPING BY

YOUR NAME:

....

IF YOU'RE NOT HERE TO SEE A MAN ABOUT A HORSE, WHAT BROUGHT YOU TO THE LOO?

☐ Just a wiz, lay off!
☐ Freshening up my make-up
☐ Escaping the crowd
☐ Letting out a secret fart or two
☐ Taking a self-guided tour
☐ Signing this stinkin' book
☐ Making a pit stop (ahem, reapplying deodorant—don't be nosy)
☐ Other:

....

DOO DOO-DLE

Draw a cute poo!

CREATE AND NAME YOUR DREAM BATHROOM FRESHENER SCENT

.... +
(Part of Speech)

.... +
(Part of Speech)

.... =
(Part of Speech)

....

MOVEMENT METER

How was your poop?

RATE YOUR POOP ON THE SCALE BELOW WITH A HAND-DRAWN POOP EMOJI:

 Dreadfully Dumpy

 Positively Poo-tastic

TOILET PAPER SUPER BOWL

Choose your battle!

CIRCLE ONE:
* SOFTEST FEEL *   * CATCHIEST JINGLE *   * HARDEST WORKING *

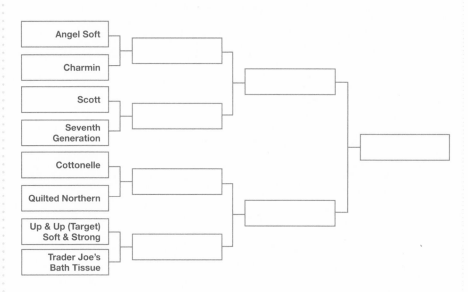

- Angel Soft
- Charmin
- Scott
- Seventh Generation
- Cottonelle
- Quilted Northern
- Up & Up (Target) Soft & Strong
- Trader Joe's Bath Tissue

.... , you're on a roll!

Winning Team

QUALITY ASS·URANCE

How did we doo-doo?

RATE YOUR EXPERIENCE ON A SCALE OF 1 TO 5, 5 MEANING EXTREMELY SATISFIED.

Cleanliness ☆ ☆ ☆ ☆ ☆

Aesthetics ☆ ☆ ☆ ☆ ☆

Toilet Paper ☆ ☆ ☆ ☆ ☆

Spray/SoapScent ☆ ☆ ☆ ☆ ☆

Privacy ☆ ☆ ☆ ☆ ☆

Ventilation ☆ ☆ ☆ ☆ ☆

Plunger Power ☆ ☆ ☆ ☆ ☆

THANKS FOR DROPPING BY

THANKS FOR DROPPING BY

YOUR NAME:

....

IF YOU'RE NOT HERE TO SEE A MAN ABOUT A HORSE, WHAT BROUGHT YOU TO THE LOO?

☐ Just a wiz, lay off!

☐ Freshening up my make-up

☐ Escaping the crowd

☐ Letting out a secret fart or two

☐ Taking a self-guided tour

☐ Signing this stinkin' book

☐ Making a pit stop (ahem, reapplying deodorant—don't be nosy)

☐ Other:

....

....

DOO DOO-DLE

Draw a cute poo!

CREATE AND NAME YOUR DREAM BATHROOM FRESHENER SCENT

.... +

(Part of Speech)

.... +

(Part of Speech)

.... =

(Part of Speech)

....

MOVEMENT METER

How was your poop?

RATE YOUR POOP ON THE SCALE BELOW WITH A HAND-DRAWN POOP EMOJI:

 Dreadfully Dumpy

 Positively Poo-tastic

TOILET PAPER SUPER BOWL

Choose your battle!

CIRCLE ONE:
* SOFTEST FEEL *   * CATCHIEST JINGLE *   * HARDEST WORKING *

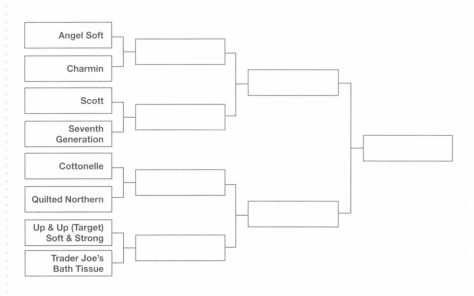

Angel Soft

Charmin

Scott

Seventh Generation

Cottonelle

Quilted Northern

Up & Up (Target) Soft & Strong

Trader Joe's Bath Tissue

...., you're on a roll!

Winning Team

QUALITY ASS-URANCE

How did we doo-doo?

RATE YOUR EXPERIENCE ON A SCALE OF
1 TO 5, 5 MEANING EXTREMELY SATISFIED.

Cleanliness ☆ ☆ ☆ ☆ ☆

Aesthetics ☆ ☆ ☆ ☆ ☆

Toilet Paper ☆ ☆ ☆ ☆ ☆

Spray/SoapScent ☆ ☆ ☆ ☆ ☆

Privacy ☆ ☆ ☆ ☆ ☆

Ventilation ☆ ☆ ☆ ☆ ☆

Plunger Power ☆ ☆ ☆ ☆ ☆

THANKS FOR DROPPING BY

THANKS FOR DROPPING BY

YOUR NAME:

....

IF YOU'RE NOT HERE TO SEE A MAN ABOUT A HORSE, WHAT BROUGHT YOU TO THE LOO?

☐ Just a wiz, lay off!

☐ Freshening up my make-up

☐ Escaping the crowd

☐ Letting out a secret fart or two

☐ Taking a self-guided tour

☐ Signing this stinkin' book

☐ Making a pit stop (ahem, reapplying deodorant—don't be nosy)

☐ Other:

....

....

DOO DOO-DLE

Draw a cute poo!

CREATE AND NAME YOUR DREAM BATHROOM FRESHENER SCENT

.... +

(Part of Speech)

.... +

(Part of Speech)

.... =

(Part of Speech)

MOVEMENT METER

How was your poop?

RATE YOUR POOP ON THE SCALE BELOW WITH A HAND-DRAWN POOP EMOJI:

 Dreadfully Dumpy

 Positively Poo-tastic

TOILET PAPER SUPER BOWL

Choose your battle!

CIRCLE ONE:
* SOFTEST FEEL *   * CATCHIEST JINGLE *   * HARDEST WORKING *

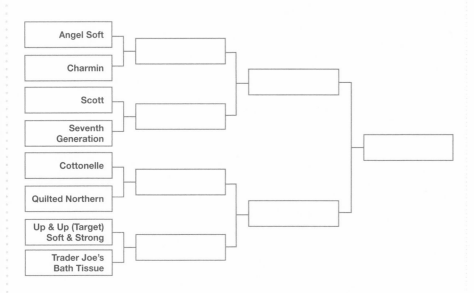

- Angel Soft
- Charmin
- Scott
- Seventh Generation
- Cottonelle
- Quilted Northern
- Up & Up (Target) Soft & Strong
- Trader Joe's Bath Tissue

.... , you're on a roll!

Winning Team

QUALITY ASS·URANCE

How did we doo-doo?

RATE YOUR EXPERIENCE ON A SCALE OF
1 TO 5, 5 MEANING EXTREMELY SATISFIED.

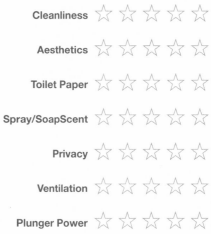

Cleanliness ☆ ☆ ☆ ☆ ☆

Aesthetics ☆ ☆ ☆ ☆ ☆

Toilet Paper ☆ ☆ ☆ ☆ ☆

Spray/SoapScent ☆ ☆ ☆ ☆ ☆

Privacy ☆ ☆ ☆ ☆ ☆

Ventilation ☆ ☆ ☆ ☆ ☆

Plunger Power ☆ ☆ ☆ ☆ ☆

THANKS FOR DROPPING BY

THANKS FOR DROPPING BY

YOUR NAME:

....

IF YOU'RE NOT HERE TO SEE A MAN ABOUT A HORSE, WHAT BROUGHT YOU TO THE LOO?

☐ Just a wiz, lay off!

☐ Freshening up my make-up

☐ Escaping the crowd

☐ Letting out a secret fart or two

☐ Taking a self-guided tour

☐ Signing this stinkin' book

☐ Making a pit stop (ahem, reapplying deodorant—don't be nosy)

☐ Other:

....

....

DOO DOO-DLE

Draw a cute poo!

CREATE AND NAME YOUR DREAM BATHROOM FRESHENER SCENT

.... +
(Part of Speech)

.... +
(Part of Speech)

.... =
(Part of Speech)

....

MOVEMENT METER

How was your poop?

RATE YOUR POOP ON THE SCALE BELOW WITH A HAND-DRAWN POOP EMOJI:

 Dreadfully Dumpy

 Positively Poo-tastic

TOILET PAPER SUPER BOWL

Choose your battle!

CIRCLE ONE:
* SOFTEST FEEL *   * CATCHIEST JINGLE *   * HARDEST WORKING *

Angel Soft

Charmin

Scott

Seventh Generation

Cottonelle

Quilted Northern

Up & Up (Target) Soft & Strong

Trader Joe's Bath Tissue

.... , you're on a roll!

Winning Team

QUALITY ASS-URANCE

How did we doo-doo?

RATE YOUR EXPERIENCE ON A SCALE OF 1 TO 5, 5 MEANING EXTREMELY SATISFIED.

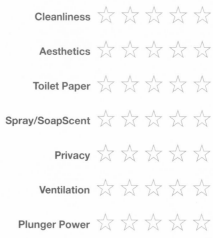

Cleanliness ☆ ☆ ☆ ☆ ☆

Aesthetics ☆ ☆ ☆ ☆ ☆

Toilet Paper ☆ ☆ ☆ ☆ ☆

Spray/SoapScent ☆ ☆ ☆ ☆ ☆

Privacy ☆ ☆ ☆ ☆ ☆

Ventilation ☆ ☆ ☆ ☆ ☆

Plunger Power ☆ ☆ ☆ ☆ ☆

THANKS FOR DROPPING BY

THANKS FOR DROPPING BY

YOUR NAME:

....

IF YOU'RE NOT HERE TO SEE A MAN ABOUT A HORSE, WHAT BROUGHT YOU TO THE LOO?

☐ Just a wiz, lay off!

☐ Freshening up my make-up

☐ Escaping the crowd

☐ Letting out a secret fart or two

☐ Taking a self-guided tour

☐ Signing this stinkin' book

☐ Making a pit stop (ahem, reapplying deodorant—don't be nosy)

☐ Other:

....

DOO DOO-DLE

Draw a cute poo!

CREATE AND NAME YOUR DREAM BATHROOM FRESHENER SCENT

.... +
(Part of Speech)

.... +
(Part of Speech)

.... =
(Part of Speech)

MOVEMENT METER

How was your poop?

RATE YOUR POOP ON THE SCALE BELOW WITH A HAND-DRAWN POOP EMOJI:

 Dreadfully Dumpy

 Positively Poo-tastic

TOILET PAPER SUPER BOWL

Choose your battle!

CIRCLE ONE:
* SOFTEST FEEL *   * CATCHIEST JINGLE *   * HARDEST WORKING *

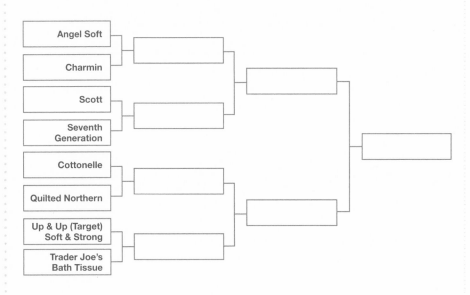

Angel Soft

Charmin

Scott

Seventh Generation

Cottonelle

Quilted Northern

Up & Up (Target) Soft & Strong

Trader Joe's Bath Tissue

.... , you're on a roll!

Winning Team

QUALITY ASS-URANCE

How did we doo-doo?

RATE YOUR EXPERIENCE ON A SCALE OF 1 TO 5, 5 MEANING EXTREMELY SATISFIED.

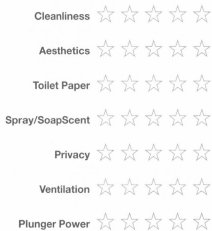

Cleanliness ☆ ☆ ☆ ☆ ☆

Aesthetics ☆ ☆ ☆ ☆ ☆

Toilet Paper ☆ ☆ ☆ ☆ ☆

Spray/SoapScent ☆ ☆ ☆ ☆ ☆

Privacy ☆ ☆ ☆ ☆ ☆

Ventilation ☆ ☆ ☆ ☆ ☆

Plunger Power ☆ ☆ ☆ ☆ ☆

THANKS FOR DROPPING BY

THANKS FOR DROPPING BY

YOUR NAME:

....

IF YOU'RE NOT HERE TO SEE A MAN ABOUT A HORSE, WHAT BROUGHT YOU TO THE LOO?

☐ Just a wiz, lay off!

☐ Freshening up my make-up

☐ Escaping the crowd

☐ Letting out a secret fart or two

☐ Taking a self-guided tour

☐ Signing this stinkin' book

☐ Making a pit stop (ahem, reapplying deodorant—don't be nosy)

☐ Other:

....

....

DOO DOO-DLE

Draw a cute poo!

CREATE AND NAME YOUR DREAM BATHROOM FRESHENER SCENT

.... +
(Part of Speech)

.... +
(Part of Speech)

.... =
(Part of Speech)

....

MOVEMENT METER

How was your poop?

RATE YOUR POOP ON THE SCALE BELOW WITH A HAND-DRAWN POOP EMOJI:

 Dreadfully Dumpy

 Positively Poo-tastic

TOILET PAPER SUPER BOWL

Choose your battle!

CIRCLE ONE:
* SOFTEST FEEL *   * CATCHIEST JINGLE *   * HARDEST WORKING *

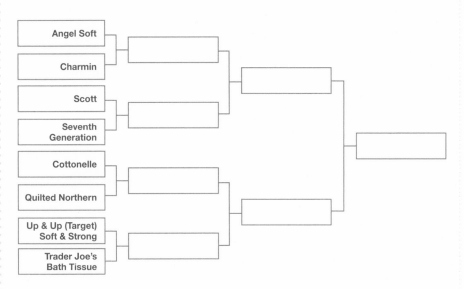

Angel Soft

Charmin

Scott

Seventh Generation

Cottonelle

Quilted Northern

Up & Up (Target) Soft & Strong

Trader Joe's Bath Tissue

.... , you're on a roll!

Winning Team

QUALITY ASS-URANCE

How did we doo-doo?

RATE YOUR EXPERIENCE ON A SCALE OF
1 TO 5, 5 MEANING EXTREMELY SATISFIED.

Cleanliness ☆ ☆ ☆ ☆ ☆

Aesthetics ☆ ☆ ☆ ☆ ☆

Toilet Paper ☆ ☆ ☆ ☆ ☆

Spray/SoapScent ☆ ☆ ☆ ☆ ☆

Privacy ☆ ☆ ☆ ☆ ☆

Ventilation ☆ ☆ ☆ ☆ ☆

Plunger Power ☆ ☆ ☆ ☆ ☆

THANKS FOR DROPPING BY

THANKS FOR DROPPING BY

YOUR NAME:

....

IF YOU'RE NOT HERE TO SEE A MAN ABOUT A HORSE, WHAT BROUGHT YOU TO THE LOO?

☐ Just a wiz, lay off!
☐ Freshening up my make-up
☐ Escaping the crowd
☐ Letting out a secret fart or two
☐ Taking a self-guided tour
☐ Signing this stinkin' book
☐ Making a pit stop (ahem, reapplying deodorant—don't be nosy)
☐ Other:

....

....

DOO DOO-DLE

Draw a cute poo!

CREATE AND NAME YOUR DREAM BATHROOM FRESHENER SCENT

.... +
(Part of Speech)

.... +
(Part of Speech)

.... =
(Part of Speech)

MOVEMENT METER

How was your poop?

RATE YOUR POOP ON THE SCALE BELOW WITH A HAND-DRAWN POOP EMOJI:

 Dreadfully Dumpy

Positively Poo-tastic

TOILET PAPER SUPER BOWL

Choose your battle!

CIRCLE ONE:
* SOFTEST FEEL *   * CATCHIEST JINGLE *   * HARDEST WORKING *

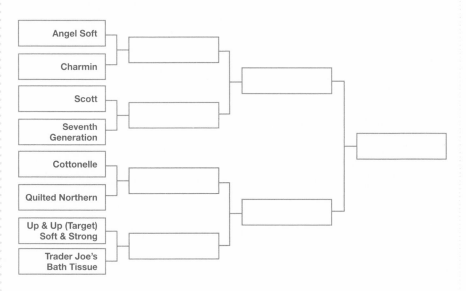

Angel Soft

Charmin

Scott

Seventh Generation

Cottonelle

Quilted Northern

Up & Up (Target) Soft & Strong

Trader Joe's Bath Tissue

.... , you're on a roll!

Winning Team

QUALITY ASS-URANCE

How did we doo-doo?

RATE YOUR EXPERIENCE ON A SCALE OF 1 TO 5, 5 MEANING EXTREMELY SATISFIED.

Cleanliness ☆ ☆ ☆ ☆ ☆

Aesthetics ☆ ☆ ☆ ☆ ☆

Toilet Paper ☆ ☆ ☆ ☆ ☆

Spray/SoapScent ☆ ☆ ☆ ☆ ☆

Privacy ☆ ☆ ☆ ☆ ☆

Ventilation ☆ ☆ ☆ ☆ ☆

Plunger Power ☆ ☆ ☆ ☆ ☆

THANKS FOR DROPPING BY

THANKS FOR DROPPING BY

YOUR NAME:

....

IF YOU'RE NOT HERE TO SEE A MAN ABOUT A HORSE, WHAT BROUGHT YOU TO THE LOO?

☐ Just a wiz, lay off!
☐ Freshening up my make-up
☐ Escaping the crowd
☐ Letting out a secret fart or two
☐ Taking a self-guided tour
☐ Signing this stinkin' book
☐ Making a pit stop (ahem, reapplying deodorant—don't be nosy)
☐ Other:

....

....

DOO DOO-DLE

Draw a cute poo!

CREATE AND NAME YOUR DREAM BATHROOM FRESHENER SCENT

.... +
(Part of Speech)

.... +
(Part of Speech)

.... =
(Part of Speech)

MOVEMENT METER

How was your poop?

RATE YOUR POOP ON THE SCALE BELOW WITH A HAND-DRAWN POOP EMOJI:

 Dreadfully Dumpy

 Positively Poo-tastic

TOILET PAPER SUPER BOWL

Choose your battle!

CIRCLE ONE:
* SOFTEST FEEL *   * CATCHIEST JINGLE *   * HARDEST WORKING *

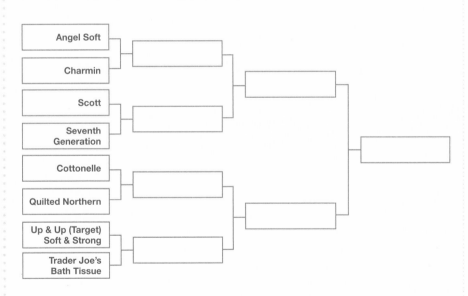

Angel Soft

Charmin

Scott

Seventh Generation

Cottonelle

Quilted Northern

Up & Up (Target) Soft & Strong

Trader Joe's Bath Tissue

.... , you're on a roll!

Winning Team

QUALITY ASS-URANCE

How did we doo-doo?

RATE YOUR EXPERIENCE ON A SCALE OF
1 TO 5, 5 MEANING EXTREMELY SATISFIED.

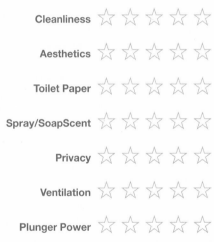

Cleanliness ☆ ☆ ☆ ☆ ☆

Aesthetics ☆ ☆ ☆ ☆ ☆

Toilet Paper ☆ ☆ ☆ ☆ ☆

Spray/SoapScent ☆ ☆ ☆ ☆ ☆

Privacy ☆ ☆ ☆ ☆ ☆

Ventilation ☆ ☆ ☆ ☆ ☆

Plunger Power ☆ ☆ ☆ ☆ ☆

THANKS FOR DROPPING BY

THANKS FOR DROPPING BY

YOUR NAME:

....

IF YOU'RE NOT HERE TO SEE A MAN ABOUT A HORSE, WHAT BROUGHT YOU TO THE LOO?

☐ Just a wiz, lay off!
☐ Freshening up my make-up
☐ Escaping the crowd
☐ Letting out a secret fart or two
☐ Taking a self-guided tour
☐ Signing this stinkin' book
☐ Making a pit stop (ahem, reapplying deodorant—don't be nosy)
☐ Other:

....

....

DOO DOO-DLE

Draw a cute poo!

CREATE AND NAME YOUR DREAM BATHROOM FRESHENER SCENT

.... +
(Part of Speech)

.... +
(Part of Speech)

.... =
(Part of Speech)

....

MOVEMENT METER

How was your poop?

RATE YOUR POOP ON THE SCALE BELOW WITH A HAND-DRAWN POOP EMOJI:

 Dreadfully Dumpy

Positively Poo-tastic

TOILET PAPER SUPER BOWL

Choose your battle!

CIRCLE ONE:
* SOFTEST FEEL *   * CATCHIEST JINGLE *   * HARDEST WORKING *

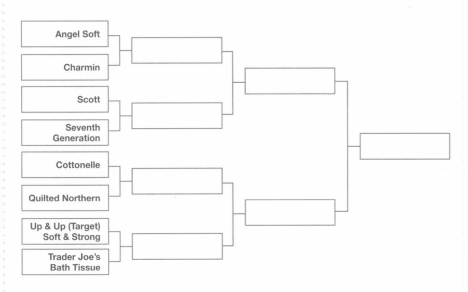

Angel Soft
Charmin
Scott
Seventh Generation
Cottonelle
Quilted Northern
Up & Up (Target) Soft & Strong
Trader Joe's Bath Tissue

...., you're on a roll!

Winning Team

QUALITY ASS·URANCE

How did we doo-doo?

RATE YOUR EXPERIENCE ON A SCALE OF
1 TO 5, 5 MEANING EXTREMELY SATISFIED.

Cleanliness ☆ ☆ ☆ ☆ ☆

Aesthetics ☆ ☆ ☆ ☆ ☆

Toilet Paper ☆ ☆ ☆ ☆ ☆

Spray/SoapScent ☆ ☆ ☆ ☆ ☆

Privacy ☆ ☆ ☆ ☆ ☆

Ventilation ☆ ☆ ☆ ☆ ☆

Plunger Power ☆ ☆ ☆ ☆ ☆

THANKS FOR DROPPING BY

THANKS FOR DROPPING BY

YOUR NAME:

....

IF YOU'RE NOT HERE TO SEE A MAN ABOUT
A HORSE, WHAT BROUGHT YOU TO THE LOO?

☐ Just a wiz, lay off!
☐ Freshening up my make-up
☐ Escaping the crowd
☐ Letting out a secret fart or two
☐ Taking a self-guided tour
☐ Signing this stinkin' book
☐ Making a pit stop (ahem, reapplying
    deodorant—don't be nosy)
☐ Other:

....

....

DOO DOO-DLE

Draw a cute poo!

CREATE AND NAME YOUR DREAM
BATHROOM FRESHENER SCENT

.... +
(Part of Speech)

.... +
(Part of Speech)

.... =
(Part of Speech)

MOVEMENT METER

How was your poop?

RATE YOUR POOP ON THE SCALE BELOW
WITH A HAND-DRAWN POOP EMOJI:

 Dreadfully Dumpy

 Positively Poo-tastic

TOILET PAPER SUPER BOWL

QUALITY ASS-URANCE

Choose your battle!

How did we doo-doo?

CIRCLE ONE:
* SOFTEST FEEL *   * CATCHIEST JINGLE *   * HARDEST WORKING *

RATE YOUR EXPERIENCE ON A SCALE OF
1 TO 5, 5 MEANING EXTREMELY SATISFIED.

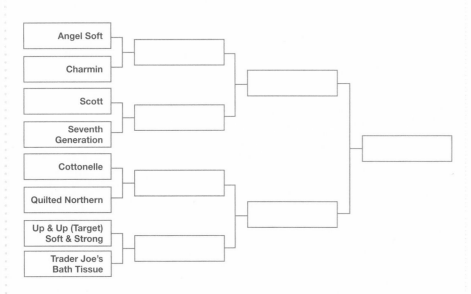

Angel Soft

Charmin

Scott

Seventh Generation

Cottonelle

Quilted Northern

Up & Up (Target) Soft & Strong

Trader Joe's Bath Tissue

Cleanliness ☆ ☆ ☆ ☆ ☆

Aesthetics ☆ ☆ ☆ ☆ ☆

Toilet Paper ☆ ☆ ☆ ☆ ☆

Spray/SoapScent ☆ ☆ ☆ ☆ ☆

Privacy ☆ ☆ ☆ ☆ ☆

Ventilation ☆ ☆ ☆ ☆ ☆

Plunger Power ☆ ☆ ☆ ☆ ☆

.... , you're on a roll!

Winning Team

THANKS FOR DROPPING BY

THANKS FOR DROPPING BY

YOUR NAME:

....

IF YOU'RE NOT HERE TO SEE A MAN ABOUT A HORSE, WHAT BROUGHT YOU TO THE LOO?

☐ Just a wiz, lay off!

☐ Freshening up my make-up

☐ Escaping the crowd

☐ Letting out a secret fart or two

☐ Taking a self-guided tour

☐ Signing this stinkin' book

☐ Making a pit stop (ahem, reapplying deodorant—don't be nosy)

☐ Other:

....

....

DOO DOO-DLE

Draw a cute poo!

CREATE AND NAME YOUR DREAM BATHROOM FRESHENER SCENT

.... +
(Part of Speech)

.... +
(Part of Speech)

.... =
(Part of Speech)

....

MOVEMENT METER

How was your poop?

RATE YOUR POOP ON THE SCALE BELOW WITH A HAND-DRAWN POOP EMOJI:

 Dreadfully Dumpy

 Positively Poo-tastic

TOILET PAPER SUPER BOWL

Choose your battle!

CIRCLE ONE:
* SOFTEST FEEL *   * CATCHIEST JINGLE *   * HARDEST WORKING *

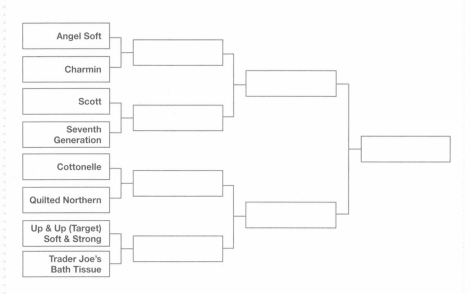

Angel Soft

Charmin

Scott

Seventh Generation

Cottonelle

Quilted Northern

Up & Up (Target) Soft & Strong

Trader Joe's Bath Tissue

...., you're on a roll!

Winning Team

QUALITY ASS-URANCE

How did we doo-doo?

RATE YOUR EXPERIENCE ON A SCALE OF 1 TO 5, 5 MEANING EXTREMELY SATISFIED.

Cleanliness ☆ ☆ ☆ ☆ ☆

Aesthetics ☆ ☆ ☆ ☆ ☆

Toilet Paper ☆ ☆ ☆ ☆ ☆

Spray/SoapScent ☆ ☆ ☆ ☆ ☆

Privacy ☆ ☆ ☆ ☆ ☆

Ventilation ☆ ☆ ☆ ☆ ☆

Plunger Power ☆ ☆ ☆ ☆ ☆

THANKS FOR DROPPING BY

HOW TO TELL IF YOUR POO IS HEALTHY

Why is my poop green? Why does my poop look like tiny rocks? These are some of the most common questions people have asked the internet and their doctors after looking at their deposits (yes, we all do it). Lucky for you, there's a system for that! Here's how it works: Check the list below. Levels 1 and 2 mean you're constipated; 3 through 5 mean your gut is good to go; and 6 and 7 mean you've got the runs.

The Bristol Stool System

1 Separate pebbly turds

2 A lumpy log

3 Sausage-y with cracks

4 Smooth and snake-like

5 Soft turdlettes

6 Mushy pieces (sorry)

7 Straight up diarrhea

FEELING CORNY?

Don't worry, corny poop is totally normal! Corn has a ton of fiber, so unless you chew a lot (like a lot, a lot) those sunny little kernels ride that log flume all the way to the end of the ride. At least you know how long it takes for your body to digest! It's like your very own science fair poo-ject.

THE BEST POO-PHEMISMS

Busting a grumpy

Communing with nature

Cutting timber

Doing the royal squat

Dropping a yam

Dropping a deuce

Dropping the kids off at the pool

Feeding the goldfish

Filling the pot

Floating a trout

Going number two

Growing a tail

Laying bricks

Laying pipe

Letting the dogs out

Logging an entry

Making a deposit

Making a sculpture

Making room for lunch

Pinching a loaf

Releasing the hounds

Seeing a man about a horse

Sinking a battleship

Sitting on the throne

Squeezing one out

Stocking the pond

Punishing the porcelain

Taking a dump

Taking care of business

Unleashing the Kraken

AN ODE TO THE BIDET

For many a year I did fear
Spraying cold water on my rear.
Then I realized what it could do
For me and you.

No more wasting lots of tissue,
And I know you won't take issue
With how clean you leave your behind,
For which you've pined.

There are many styles and brands,
So don't deny your butt's demands
And find yourself a good bidet.
Do it today.

There isn't much more to be said,
So don't leave your booty on read.
Just do yourself a big favor
And be braver.

SQUATTY SONNET

I have never quite felt such a pleasure
As when using this amazing device,
Which lets me go with so little pressure
And helps my bathroom time remain concise.

Now that I have this lavatory stool,
I must say my life is very much improved.
My bottom agrees that it is a jewel,
And my bowels so smoothly are moved.

Without this helpful contraption I fear
That others are miserably lacking
In such a delight that could draw a tear
While they would be so happily slacking.

For anyone who does not love this tool
Must be the biggest, constipated fool.

STERLING

New York

An Imprint of Sterling Publishing Co., Inc.

STERLING and the distinctive Sterling logo
are registered trademarks of Sterling Publishing Co., Inc.

© 2022 Sterling Publishing Co., Inc.
Text by Gabrielle Van Tassel

ISBN 978-1-4549-4523-9

Distributed in Canada by Sterling Publishing Co., Inc.
c/o Canadian Manda Group, 664 Annette Street
Toronto, Ontario M6S 2C8, Canada
Distributed in the United Kingdom by GMC Distribution Services
Castle Place, 166 High Street, Lewes, East Sussex BN7 1XU, England
Distributed in Australia by NewSouth Books
University of New South Wales, Sydney, NSW 2052, Australia

For information about custom editions, special sales, and premium and corporate purchases,
please contact Sterling Special Sales at specialsales@sterlingpublishing.com.

Manufactured in China

2 4 6 8 10 9 7 5 3 1

sterlingpublishing.com

Image Credits: CanStockPhoto: hayatikayhan (empty roll), Getty Images: CNuisin/iStock/Getty Images Plus (icon),
Shutterstock.com: Muilee (corn emoji); Irina Strelnikova (poo emojis)